Walter Besant

This Son of Vulcan

Vol. III

Walter Besant

This Son of Vulcan
Vol. III

ISBN/EAN: 9783337041076

Printed in Europe, USA, Canada, Australia, Japan

Cover: Foto ©ninafisch / pixelio.de

More available books at **www.hansebooks.com**

THIS SON OF VULCAN.

A Novel.

BY THE AUTHORS OF
"READY-MONEY MORTIBOY," "MY LITTLE GIRL,"
"WITH HARP AND CROWN," "THE CASE OF MR. LUCRAFT,"
"THE GOLDEN BUTTERFLY," ETC., ETC.

IN THREE VOLUMES.
VOL. III.

LONDON:
SAMPSON LOW, MARSTON, SEARLE & RIVINGTON,
CROWN BUILDINGS, 188, FLEET STREET.
1876.

(All rights reserved.)

PART THE SECOND.

(Continued.)

THIS SON OF VULCAN.

CHAPTER X.

But Jack returned no more to the works. Next morning he called very early to see Mr. Bayliss, who was at breakfast.

Ella was pouring out tea, and made a pretty picture in her light morning dress and fair curls.

"Come in, Armstrong," shouted Mr. Bayliss, in his cheeriest way, "come in. Hodder was here last night. And I'm going to make an example of every man. Hodder's got the names of some fifty. You may trust Hodder in everything that doesn't want more than common sense. Sit down and have some breakfast."

"Oh! Mr. Armstrong," said Ella, in her pretty, placid way, "we have heard the whole story. And you might have been killed."

"Might have been killed? Would have been killed," said her father, "but for that trump of a girl, Norah Cuolahan. Countess of Connaught, Frank Perrymont calls her. Gad! I'd make her Duchess at once, if I had my will. To think of her—Hodder met her, and told her he was afraid there would be danger. Instead of sending for the police, she made Hodder take her to the place. She ought to be a general in petticoats. Armstrong, I drink her health in a cup of tea."

"Norah is a brave girl," said Jack, reddening.

"Will you take tea or coffee, Mr. Armstrong?" asked Ella. "Oh! how I wish I had been there! To do one brave thing in your life, you know; it makes one envious. Two lumps of sugar or one? Three? oh! Mr. Armstrong, that is very extravagant. I should like to have seen Norah as Hodder described her. Papa, I didn't know before that Hodder was so clever."

"Hodder is mad about it, Jack. He was

here last night describing the whole scene; and if I did not know that Hodder is the most sober creature alive, I should have said he had been drinking. As it is, I can only say that Hodder has mistaken his vocation, and ought to have been an actor."

"And when she took the wretched man away from the mob, where did she take him to?"

"She took him to the Cottage, and gave him something to eat. Then he went away and disappeared," said Jack. "But it was not to talk about Norah that I came up, Mr. Bayliss. It was to ask you a favour."

"Ask a dozen, my boy, and you shall have them all. I was in hopes that you were going to show me the invention that they made so much of."

"Not yet, Mr. Bayliss. I will come to that presently."

"Well, let us talk business. Ella, my girl, run away and blow up the servants. She always does that every morning."

"Oh, papa!" And ran away.

"Now then, Armstrong."

"First, I want you to forgive the hands,

who were goaded to madness by that miserable fellow, Cardiff."

"Never, by the Lord! Out they go!"

"You see, Mr. Bayliss, there are four hundred of them. You can't punish all. One is as guilty as the other, if there is any guilt. And the man had deceived them all with his lies."

"What did Cuolahan mean by ever letting you be mixed up with such a rascal?"

"I will tell you the story as briefly as I can."

Jack told him, beginning from the time when he left the house of the Bastables.

"The man is gone. It is my belief that he will never come back again. The cause removed, the effect has already disappeared, and the hands were as demonstrative with me in the popular direction as they were in the other."

"Forgive them?" said Mr. Bayliss meditatively. "Forgive them? Well; it was not my intention, I assure you. But as you ask it—you are the aggrieved party—I don't well see how I can refuse you. I will have them up, and make them a speech, this very morning."

"Thank you. Now there is another thing. It is more than a year since I was out of my apprenticeship. I have worked on in your engine-room, waiting for something to turn up, and nothing has yet turned up."

"Well—no," said his employer, to whom Jack was a servant whom he got for nothing. "I have not yet seen my way—but I shall before long, I have no doubt I shall—to offering you a regular salary and a leading position. I have not forgotten that in the old days your poor father and I were partners. It was a sorry business we had, Armstrong; a devilish poor affair, as you may guess. Only the finding of the iron set me up."

"That, and the working of the Ravendale seam, I suppose."

"Ay—ay!" returned Mr. Bayliss. "That was the best stroke of business I ever did. But go on."

"What I came especially to say is this: Mr. Fortescue, with his usual liberality, wants me to go to Germany."

"Go to Germany? What will you see in Germany that you cannot see here?"

"Not much. Our machinery is better; our

men are better; and where they work one ton, we work a thousand. Still, there is something. Where is the finest steel made?"

"In Prussia, confound it!"

"Yes; but why?"

"You ought to know by this time."

"I do know. But I want to go and see. I am a chemist, as you know, among other things."

"You are a devilish clever young fellow, Jack Armstrong," said Mr. Bayliss. "And you know everything, I believe."

"I know a good deal about metals. And I am going to Germany to learn more. I am going to find out, Mr. Bayliss," said Jack, his face flushing, "if I can, the way to make as good steel here as they make in Prussia."

Bayliss looked at him for a moment with a sort of astonishment.

"By Gad! you are a plucky young rascal. And ambitious, I believe."

"I told you before that I am ambitious. Mr. Bayliss, all this town, and all the land around it, once belonged to my fathers." Mr. Bayliss turned pale. "That is all gone now, and gone for good." Mr. Bayliss recovered his natural colour. "But I cannot bear to think that I shall have to go on all my life as an *employé*. I tell you because you are an old friend of my father's, and because you have been extremely kind to me, that I mean to be a master. Mr. Fortescue talks of giving me money, but I have no claims to it, and he has cousins who will think that I have defrauded them. I would rather make my own way."

"It is an honourable ambition, Jack," replied Mr. Bayliss. "A very honourable ambition. It was my own. 'Let me make my own way,' I used to say, 'and show the world what sort of a man I am.' Go on, even if you clash with my interests."

"I shall hardly do that," said Jack.

"I don't know. I am not so young as I was. I am fifty. I have no successor. Perhaps—who knows? And then you will marry Norah Cuolahan, I suppose?"

It was Jack's turn to change colour.

"I am afraid not. I am sure I shall not. I have always regarded Norah as my sister."

"And as for a successor," continued Mr. Bayliss, in a ruminative manner, "I suppose you know, or, if you do not, I may tell you in confidence, that I have always looked on the marriage of my daughter and Frank Perrymont as the most natural way of carrying on my works. Frank has not your practical abilities, but he will learn, and, after all, the ball once set rolling is kept up by the paid people whose interest it is. The work is, you know, enormous—enormous," he added, with a succulent roll of his tongue. "But we capitalists are never content. Suppose I may be worth a few hundreds of thousands now, why should I not be worth a few millions? Jack Armstrong, you will get in the swim presently, for you are a fellow of determination—got it from your mother, I suppose."

"Was my poor mother possessed of determination?"

"She must have been, or else she never could have——" ("married your father," he was going to say, but he checked himself)—"never could have given birth to you, my boy. However, let us return to business. You will go to Germany, you say. Very good. I cannot stop you. When do you return?"

"I propose to be away for a twelvemonth

or so. Meantime, I am anxious about Myles
Cuolahan. Will you keep him on?"

"Armstrong, Cuolahan is the most honest
collector I ever had, and the most regular.
The rents come in, thanks to his blarney,
with twice the certainty they used to. I shall
keep him on, and I shall raise his salary.
The rents," he said, "are a small matter to
me, of course, but it is my principle, even
over a thousand or two a year, to have things
as carefully managed as with the great works.
Cuolahan shall stay."

"Thank you. It would break the poor
fellow's heart, now that he has his daughter
with him, to give up his new life and take
to the old. That, however, would be impossible."

"And Miss Ferens?"

"Miss Ferens acquiesces in everything.
More than that, she finds she cannot live
altogether apart from Norah, and talks of
staying with her sometimes."

"Indeed! Really, I am astonished. We
shall be glad to call upon Miss Ferens. I am
very glad indeed to learn that we are going to
have Miss Ferens at Esbrough. And when
do you start, Armstrong?"

"I start as soon as I can get away—as soon as you will let me go."

"I will not keep you a minute. I discharge you," said Bayliss, laughing. "I discharge you from this moment. And, my dear boy, if my purse can——"

"Thank you very much," said Jack; "but I only take money from Mr. Fortescue. He always keeps me well supplied. And now, Mr. Bayliss, that I have got your promise to forgive the hands, and to keep on Myles Cuolahan in your employment, and have obtained my discharge from the works, I think there is nothing more to say, except to thank you again. Forgive me for keeping my invention a secret. It is intended to lay the foundation-stone of my fortune."

They shook hands and parted. Bayliss, when he was gone, sat thinking. The past was twelve years old and more; it was well-nigh forgotten; there was little remorse, pity, or fear left after so many years of safety and unsuspicion. He held the land which he had fraudulently acquired; on it was the seam of iron, and on it stood the works out of which he had built a gigantic fortune : but he forgot how he had acquired it. It is not true, you see, that criminals are always shaking in their shoes. I believe that they go on comfortably enough so long as the prospect of being found out is remote. When the chance appears probable, they repent and are exceedingly sorry, just like the bad boy at the approach of the cane. The law seemed far off to Mr. Bayliss, and indeed he had almost ceased to believe in its existence. But this young Armstrong. He began to think that he was getting old. Supposing Frank Perrymont and Ella were to marry. The great works could never be improved unless in more vigorous hands. This young Armstrong, this clever, fearless, confident young fellow, who marched straight on to his goal, whatever it was—why not marry him to Ella, instead? And then, as he thought of the lad's determined face and resolute step, he thought of what might happen if——but no, that was impossible. Armstrong went back to the Cottage. Norah was alone, for her father had gone about his collecting business. She was at some light work, sitting among her flowers and singing softly to herself.

Jack sat down opposite to her, and was silent.

"You are taking a holiday, Jack?" she asked. "All wheels and whirr makes Jack a dull boy. You shall walk with me as far as High Street presently, if you like."

"I am going away, Norah."

"Going away? Oh, Jack! Going away? And when?"

"I am only going for a few months, because —for several reasons. Partly because I cannot go back and work among the men as I have done. I have grown out of it, Norah. And there is another thing: I want to follow up an idea."

"More wheels, Jack? Oh! when will you think about something else?"

"What is better to think about, Norah? Mr. Fortescue approves entirely, and I am going to Germany."

"And leave me, Jack? Leave my father and me alone?"

Jack's heart gave a mighty heave. Among the wheels that filled his brain there was always Norah's face; amid the din of the engines, above the awful thud of the steam hammer, and louder than the shriek of the whistle, was the sweet, soft voice of Norah. Not one of those voices that pretend to be soft, and so are spoken low; but a voice that was loud and clear as a bell, and yet always soft; as soft when it rang out with a fighting song, as when it wept in an Irish ballad. Leave Norah? It was hard.

"Leave us both, Jack?"

"Yes, Norah. I have been very happy since you came. So happy, but for one thing, that I do not feel the same man."

"What is the one thing, Jack?"

"I will tell you, some day. In fact, I suppose I must. Yes, Norah, I am going to Germany; and I shall stay six months, a year, two years, as long as I have to stay until my problem is worked out. It is a great problem, Norah, and one that will bring me fortune, if I solve it."

"You do not love money, Jack?"

"Yes I do, Norah. I love money for the things it will bring. I should like to put you into a better house, and to let your father do nothing all his life but admire you; and——"

"And what would you do with yourself, Jack?"

"I have got nothing to do with myself," said Jack gloomily. "I am done for already."

Then he began to trifle round the room, taking up little things and putting them down again, hovering round the girl like a moth round a lamp. She sat half watching him, waiting for him to speak, but working away still, after the way of her sex, with the air of being deeply occupied with the embroidery.

Her hair, lustrous and dark; the soft splendour of her eyes; the bend of her neck; the divine shape of her head; her pretty fingers deftly working in and out among the threads; the music of her voice; the rustle of her dress; all these were so many magnets which had attracted the unhappy young man till he could bear it no longer. It was not his desire to work out a problem which drove him away; it was not his invention which kept him night after night among his wheels; it was not thought of mechanics which made him silent and gloomy; it was Norah—Norah and the other woman; the siren who had lulled him with flatteries, beguiled him with music, persuaded him that she was beautiful and good, and coaxed his troth from him.

He stood over her, and he noticed that her fingers trembled as she worked; for if he dared not speak to her, she dared not look up at him.

He lost his self-control; he stooped and took her hand in his; he knelt at her feet, and kissed it passionately.

"I am breaking my honour in speaking to you. I have no right to tell you that I love you, Norah."

"No right, Jack? Why have you no right?"

"Because, Norah, you will hate me. Because I have given away my word to another woman. Because I was a poor foolish creature, who allowed himself to be cajoled and tricked. Norah, I love you, and I am engaged to another woman. Pity me."

Norah's tears rose to her eyes. Then she gently withdrew her hand, and tried to face the question.

"Jack," she whispered, "is it Ella Bayliss?"

"No," he answered.

She was silent again for a space.

"Jack, is there no way out of it?"

"None."

"Does she know that you do not love her?"

"She knows. But she will not give me up. Do not ask me any more, Norah."

"She knows, and she will not give him up," Norah repeated. "Jack, let us have no concealments." She placed her hand on his arm. "I love you too. I know it now. I knew it the moment I felt the touch of your hand and your lips on my hand. I love you as much as you can love me, and more, my own, my hero—more a thousand times, because you have your work to think about, and I have only—you. My poor Jack, we are very unhappy. How old was I when Miss Ferens took me away?"

"I don't know, Norah. Four or five. Such a little thing. Such an affectionate little girl, with your arms round my neck always. And I was only eight or nine. We slept on the same bed—a rough, coarse bed it was, but we lay in each other's arms. I have never thought about it until now, because I have always been so hard at work. Now it all comes back to me, the old time."

"I remember a little, Jack, and all these years I have had you before my eyes. I thought of your growing up, and growing wise—my father told me all when he came every year to see me—we used to talk about nothing but you. I knew all about your pony, and your books, and how Mr. Fortescue taught you. And so, somehow, you were always present with me. When Miss Ferens and I came to understand each other, I told her all, and she was jealous of you, because she loved me so much herself. Let us tell each other everything. You will not think me . . . unmaidenly, will you, Jack, if I tell you all?"

"Norah!"

"Then my father asked me to come home to him, and I came. It was right to come; but, Jack—I could only confess it to you—the thought was in my mind that I should meet you again. And I came. You were so cold, Jack, when first I came."

"It was because I was afraid of you, Norah."

"Afraid of me? Oh, Jack, how could you be afraid of me?"

"You were so much above me. You were so different to the young ladies I had ever seen before. You were——"

"No, Jack, not above you. Only different from you. I see, now, that we have been brought up to look at things from different points of view. That is not being above you."

"Norah, you do not know all."

"Then do not tell me all. And when my father kissed me, Jack, I turned to be kissed by my brother, and he only gave me a timid pressure of his fingers. Then I knew that we were no longer brother and sister, and the old relations disappeared. I tried to keep it up, Jack, but it would not do."

"No, Norah, it would not do. A veil has come up between us two. My dear, there is always a veil between two people who love each other, till they know the truth, and then the veil is taken off."

"Yes, Jack!" She made a little motion with both her hands, as if to shake off a veil from her face. "See, Jack, the veil has gone. Read me now! Read my very soul, if you will."

She laid her arm round his neck, and her face to his, for all this time Jack was kneeling at her feet. He drew her to him and kissed her, not passionately, but sadly.

"Should I have told you, darling?" he whispered. "Is it not a double breach of faith?"

"No, Jack! I thank God that you have told me. Now I shall be happier. Tell me one thing, Jack. Is *she* in Germany?"

"No, Norah."

"Then go, Jack! go! It will give us time. Let me kiss you once, just as if I were a little girl again."

She half rose from her chair and threw herself before him, her arms round his neck, her cheek against his. It was so like, and so unlike, the last embrace that Jack had received from Mrs. Merrion, that his heart fell like lead.

Then she rose. Jack rose, too, and they stood face to face, hand-locked.

"You see, Jack, now, that I love you. I shall always love you. If you cannot marry me, Jack, never mind. That is nothing, now that I know that we love each other. But if anything goes wrong with you, Jack—if you are ever troubled, ever anxious, ever despondent about things which are not those of your wedded life, remember that I always love you, and that you must come to me. Promise me, dear Jack."

"I promise, Norah."

"Jack, you will be vexing yourself that you have told me. Do not, dear. It is better so. It is better always to know the truth, and face it; and then we can do our duty. You will try to give up thinking of me, and then you will perhaps get to think of, and love—the other one——"

"Norah, I am always thinking of her. And the more I think, the less I love her."

"Jack, I saw the other day, quoted, two lines which seem to me the noblest that English gentleman ever wrote. Do you know them?—

'I could not love thee, dear, so much,
  Loved I not honour more.'"

"I know," said Jack. "Norah, I am glad I told you."

"Yes," said Norah, "you have loved me. That will be always something to think about.

Only, Jack, henceforth it must never be spoken of again. I have had my love-scene. I have told you all. Ask me any question you like, and I will answer it. But we must never again speak of love. For that is a secret between us that must be hidden away for ever."

"You are always right, Norah," said Jack. "If you knew how contemptible I feel in your eyes, how wretched in my own, you would—— "

"Nonsense, Jack! I should do nothing. You must not feel contemptible. I ask you nothing. But I shall very soon know everything. You will go to Germany. You will work. You will make yourself famous. Perhaps—who knows?—you may escape from the fetters that bind you. And then we can talk again. But my Jack will always save his honour."

Jack said nothing, but kissed her hand humbly, and left the room.

Norah heard him go into his study and lock the door, and then she crept upstairs, and threw herself upon the bed, crying and sobbing. Jack loved her—but of what use was his love when he was promised to another? Who was that other? She started from the bed, and stood thinking. As she stood, she heard Jack's feet in the little hall. He left the house. She darted to the window, just to look at him. She saw him step across the road, and stop for a moment irresolute at the door of Laburnum Cottage. Then he walked up the steps and knocked.

Norah sank back against the wall. Good heavens! He was going to marry Mrs. Merrion.

There was no doubt in her mind, not the least. She had found out the truth. All in a moment it flashed upon her. The other one —the woman he was engaged to marry—it was Mrs. Merrion. She divined the truth: she *felt* that she was right. Marry Mrs. Merrion? "Not," thought Norah, "if I can prevent it."

Then she sat down to think. She wept no more. The spirit of war was in her breast; she must fight for her lover; she must, somehow, rescue him. But how? She did not know.

Should she tell her father? No. Should

she tell Miss Ferens? Yes: but it would be of little use. Should she tell Mr. Fortescue? Perhaps.

Mrs. Bastable—it suddenly flashed across her how Mrs. Bastable once mysteriously hinted at things going on which she should not allow to advance beyond a certain point— that was Jack's involvement.

"He *shall* not marry her!" said the girl, setting her lips together and flashing her eyes. "He is mine."

You may inflict all wrongs upon a woman, and she will forgive you—except three. You may not forsake her for another woman; you may not take away her child; and you may not take away her lover.

CHAPTER XI.

JACK's departure, and the knowledge that he loved her, was to Norah like the removal of the sun from her sky. Life grew grey, colourless, and clouded. It was bad in the morning to rise with the consciousness that there would be no Jack all day long, but it was worse in the long evenings, which she passed chiefly with her father. Poor Myles had improved himself, taking the hugest pains, and no longer offended in small matters. But he was afraid of his daughter. It seemed to him something inexplicable that he should be the progenitor of such a girl: he lived in a perennial condition of awe and wonder: she belonged to another world; and though he tried to be grateful for so many mercies, he was also constrained in her presence. At morning and at evening he kissed her with a sweet caress to which his memory loved to turn. But he could not make it out. She talked to him, but her talk was different to Jack's: she poured into his mind ideas that made him ashamed of his crude notions, for he was quick at catching new things, like all Irishmen: she looked after him: she loved him—that was the strangest thing of any. And now that Jack was gone Norah would sit with him while he smoked his pipes—and yet his evenings seemed lonely. For Myles Cuolahan looked on his daughter as a veritable goddess. He had become accustomed to think of her as something so very different in his solitary days and nights; and now that he had her with him always he lost the very materials of thought, for she was a reality to him. The house was silent for want of Jack's step: it was gloomy for want of Jack's laugh: it was melancholy for want of Jack to keep them talking. And then, a fresh complication to poor Myles's troubles, came Miss Ferens. She did not, as she proposed at first, give up her house at Bedesbury, but she came to Esbrough and took lodgings for a time. And she always seemed to be in the house, this woman with the earnest eyes and the deep voice, in whose presence poor Myles could never force himself to say a word.

Norah told Miss Ferens everything.

"He loves me," the girl said, with sparkling eyes. "Why should he love me—he so clever and I so ignorant? How happy and grateful I ought to be! I seem to care nothing that he has made it impossible for us ever to marry —for oh! it is so pleasant to feel that one is loved. I wonder why Jack loves me—I forgot to ask him. You see we only talked about it for half an hour, and then we had so much to say that it went out of my head."

"He loves you, my dear," said Miss Ferens in her harsh voice, "because you are beautiful; and men always fancy beautiful women are angels. You are a good girl, my Norah, but you are not an angel."

"Am I pretty? I never thought much about it till I came here. Ella Bayliss says I am. But love cannot have everything to do with beauty."

"No, dear. I suppose not; though I know little enough about it. No man ever paid any attention to me, as I have often told you. But of one thing I am quite sure, that no really ugly woman was ever yet loved by any man. My dear, if a man wants to marry he must get money: if a woman wants to marry she must get good looks."

"But it sounds degrading to us that we are only to be loved for what we cannot help."

"Yes, dear; there are a good many things in life that take the conceit out of us: having to get old, being neglected, having to die, whether you like it or not—all these things are degrading. But on the whole I don't think it is degrading to be loved for one's beauty first of all—if one can convert the fire of a passion into a lasting flame. Norah, dear, I am as sure as a loveless woman can be of anything that there is no greater gift to our sex than the steady love of a man. Woe to her that has it and throws it away! You have got it, my dear, even though it be only like the spring blossom, that comes and falls and leaves no fruit behind. It will be something to make you happier all your life."

"I know who it is," said Norah, reddening, "at least I guess. Oh! I *know*, because I feel it. It is Mrs. Merrion, that woman of whom I wrote to you. I hate her, Miss Ferens. Do not tell me just now that it is unchristian, because I cannot help it. I hate her. She is twelve years older than poor Jack: she paints her withered cheeks: she dyes her hair: she wears false curls: she enamels her wrinkled forehead: she——"

"Norah!" cried Miss Ferens. "Stop, child—stop! Where have you learned all these things?"

"Ella Bayliss told me," answered Norah, subdued. "Ella hates her too, because—oh! Miss Ferens, it seems too wicked—the dreadful woman allows Mr. Bayliss and Captain Perrymont to visit her."

"Well, Norah, why not? She cannot marry everybody, you know."

"Please don't talk about her any more, Miss Ferens. It makes me feel out of peace with the world and everybody in it."

The odd thing was that the day after Jack went away Mrs. Merrion herself disappeared, taking with her the French maid, and leaving

Mrs. Bastable in charge of the house. This good woman, being quite alone, began to make little deferential visits to Norah, ostensibly to ask after Mr. Armstrong. She came in the morning when Norah was sure to be alone and able to receive her. In consideration of her interest in Jack, Norah forgave her connection with the enemy and allowed her to talk. She wandered a good deal when she did talk.

"I remember his father and mother, Miss Cuolahan, all the same as if it was yesterday. Poor Johnny Armstrong hadn't much left of the property that he and his father, and his grandfather too, had all been making ducks and drakes of. Partner he was of Mr. Bayliss, and they'd got a little scrap factory—quite a poor thing. It was before my Benjamin came to the town, and I've been married twenty years and been separated—that is, I've been neither wife nor maid nor widow, if you call that being separated—for twelve years and more. All Johnny had left—because his wife told me a month before the dreadful fire, and she near her time—was a field; the very field where Mr. Bayliss's works stand. That

was all; and when he died there was nothing,
and no relations. Mr. Bayliss behaved handsome, and gave poor Johnny and his wife a
decent funeral, poor as he was. And then
your mother—Lord! Miss Norah, it's
wonderful that you should be her daughter—
she took Jack and brought him up, and they
went away, and I never set eyes on him again,
till he came to live with me."

"Yes, I know about it!"

"Ah! Benjamin had found me out by that
time. When we first kept company he was a
lawyer's clerk; come from Newcastle, he told
me, for I never knew any of his friends: and
when we married he got a berth in London,
and we went to town to live: that was twenty
years ago. But then he got into bad hands,
at least"—she corrected herself—"I never
speak harm of the sperruts; for he found out
his own powers and mine too. Miss Norah,
many's the time I've read my Bible and got
no comfort from it, but only wretchedness and
misery. For the leaves open always in one or
two places. There's the place where it says,
'A man or a woman that hath a familiar
sperrut, or that is a wizard, shall surely be

put to death.' My dear, I'm sure my husband and me had a hundred sperruts, all on familiar terms. There's the story of the woman of Endor who called up Samuel. I don't know about him, and I never called him; but I've called up Peters, and Pauls, and Johns by the dozen; and they came: and much good I got out of it, or my husband either. And the wickedness of it. My dear, did you ever hear of a rich witch? No! nor ever will. I've been a witch, and so I ought to know. And it's among the works of the flesh, put with idolatry, envy, hatred, and all the other dreadful things. And so the rest of the Bible seems no good to me."

"But how have you been a witch?"

"Don't ask me, young lady, for I can't tell you. It was Benjamin's doing. He found me out, and then I had no peace of my life. He threw me into trances whenever he pleased, and then I could see everything that went on everywhere. Pray, my dear, that you may not be a clairvoyong. And the rappings that went on; the fingers you felt in your hair at night, and the things you saw! Sometimes I think that the power has gone out of me, for I don't feel now as I used to, long after Benjamin went away and left me. Then I knew when he was thinking of me by the terrors that fell on me; and I followed him in a trance. He went across the sea in a ship; I saw him in a great town; after that, I saw him now and then, but each time more feebly, till at last it went out of my power altogether. I don't think he's dead, my dear. But, oh! to think of him coming back, after all these years, and beginning the old carryings on."

"Is Mrs. Merrion his cousin?"

"No, Miss Cuolahan, Jenny's my own cousin."

"Jenny? I thought her name was Adelaide."

Mrs. Bastable put up her two hands in a serious way, and whispered:

"Hush, Miss Cuolahan! Never you mention it to a soul, please, but her name is Jenny, plain Jane Susan, as ever was."

"And she is your cousin?"

"Not born here, but away in Shropshire. Yes! my mother's sister's daughter. She's got money and I've got none. So I live with her, and do for her. She's mad because the Esbrough ladies won't call upon her; but as I tell her, and it makes her mad, 'You know, Jenny, you never was a real lady, and a nursery governess is very well to begin with, but it doesn't make a young woman a countess all at once.' She can't bear being called Jenny, you know. And I think it's because I can't help it, for the name is as pat in my head as the grace before meat, and Adelaide is too outlandish, that I've got to stay downstairs when there's company. Jenny always says I'm out, but that's rubbish. I make the dinner. But she's a dreadful temper, my dear Miss Cuolahan, and it's a terrible time I have with her, one way and the other, and only my own sister's family in the world to go to if I leave Jenny, and they too poor to help me. Well! we've all got our burdens, and when it's over we shall be thinking of what we've received, and not what we haven't had. There's gentlemen call on Jenny enough, I'm sure. Mr. Bayliss drops in of a night and stays talking; and Captain Perrymont, he's taken to coming of an evening too, to say nothing of Mr. Armstrong. See, Miss Norah, Mr. Armstrong's there too often—now, mind I told you so. You keep him away."

"He is in Germany, now, at any rate."

"And none of them ever come in the same evening, which shows how clever she is. There's more, too; but never mind; only it grieves me to see poor young Mr. Armstrong dragged in with the rest. I told her so the other day. I said, 'Jenny, do what you like with the old ones. There's Mr. Bayliss, with his fat, red face, and Captain Perrymont, with his thin, white face. You can make fools of them, if you like. But you don't make a fool of Jack Armstrong, or, as sure as my name is Keziah Bastable, I'll stop it.' I told her that, plump. And then she flew into one of her rages."

"You told her that?" asked Norah with flashing eyes.

"Miss Cuolahan, I'll tell you something else. I'm only a weak, silly woman, and my nerves all gone to pieces with the clairvoyonging, but I've my feelings like women that haven't been sinful witches. And once I loved Johnny Armstrong, your Jack's father.

It wasn't the like of me that an Armstrong would marry, though they were down in the world. Not but what ours was a respectable family as any in Esbrough, and my father parish clerk for thirty years; but we weren't Armstrongs, you know, we were only Kislingburys. You see the Kislingburys' headstones in the old churchyard, but the Armstrongs are mostly buried in the church, as they should, among the quality. It was a Kislingbury that built the parish pump, and an Armstrong that paid for it—well! I was young and foolish, and Johnny Armstrong used to meet me at nights, and—there—it seemed nothing that he should put his arm round my waist, you know, and kiss me; and he meant nothing, and I thought he meant everything. It's the way of men. I couldn't cry, because I had no place to cry in, not even at night, when I slept with my sister. And when I married Bastable, I re'lly believe it was because I wanted to think over handsome Johnny Armstrong, married, and dead, and buried, and to cry over him when I was alone."

She stopped, out of breath.

"And now I'll go," she said. "You won't

say a word of what I told you, Miss Cuolahan? Promise me! It would take the bread out of my mouth if you did. Shh-sh!" she whispered, "*Jenny hates you.* But don't you mind. I've got her tight, and she knows it. She's coming back next month."

Mrs. Bastable gone, Norah breathed more freely. She began to put things together. There was, then, something wrong about this woman. She called herself by a false name: she deceived people, so far. And though the prattling Bastable woman was as shallow as a mountain brook and as disconnected as a racked heretic, there was no doubt that she had power over her cousin and meant to use it. So Norah felt some of the weight off her mind. Should she tell Jack? Should she tell Miss Ferens?

She told the latter, at all events. But Miss Ferens was new to such things as wicked or intriguing women, and could advise nothing, except that Mrs. Bastable should tell Jack on his return.

Meantime there were festivities at which Miss Ferens was welcome as one who belonged to the best Bedesbury circles as well as the guardian of the Countess of Connaught. The autumn was a time that brought many visitors to Esbrough and its neighbourhood. In Ravendale county, as they called it, was the seat of the great and wealthy Earl of Ravendale, a baronet or two, with half a dozen squires of good old family; then a clergyman, like Mr. Fortescue, who was also a gentleman by birth and a scholar : these gave society in the neighbourhood of Esbrough its hall-mark. And into those circles Paul Bayliss, Mayor, J.P., chairman of everything, had not yet penetrated. He wanted his daughter to be one of the county ladies. He wanted to see himself invited in Ravendale county. First, he tried to get in by means of Captain Perrymont, whose interests were bound up with his own in so many ways. That could not be managed on account of the Captain's reserve, Bayliss said—really because the Captain thought his quasi partner vulgar, as indeed he was. But Bayliss became less vulgar. He did not brandish his wealth in people's faces; he put on comparatively quiet manners; he could not help keeping himself in the front, but it was more with the air of one who has been born to greatness, such as that with which we might expect of the son—say of Lord Derby. The later manner of Paul Bayliss was rather good. He learned not to affect, not to parade, not to conceal—three very valuable lessons to a *parvenu*. Then Mr. Fortescue, who liked the man for a shrewd common sense, which contrasted with his secluded and scholarly habits but yet did not jar with them, took him up, and would drive over to the Hall to the great dinners. Presently the great dinners—perhaps through Ella's influence—became smaller and quieter; though Bayliss, with a sense of fitness which was almost artistic, refused to lessen the magnificence of service. The big red-faced successful man with the loud full voice seemed in his place behind an immense priceless épergne, and in the midst of gold and silver plate. He liked it: he felt it due to his position as a millionaire. He told Miss Ferens, truly enough, that if he were a man of good birth whose money had descended to him, he should make no show. "As it is," he said, "my money is all that recommends me—so I show it. I was just as able, just as great a man before I had my money as I am now, only, you see, people had not found it out then. It's the framing, Miss Ferens, that makes many a picture look handsome. And I'm so splendidly framed that, by George, most people take me for a picture by one of the old masters."

"Indeed!" said Miss Ferens, laughing in her deep voice. "You are something like a Rubens I have seen."

Miss Ferens and Norah stayed at the Hall for a fortnight. A Baronet called, and stayed to dinner. More than that, the Baronet asked them all to dine, and had a Lord in his house. So that Paul Bayliss began to think that, after all, he was going to belong to the upper circles. It did not seem to give Ella as much gratification as her father. Indeed, the conduct of that young lady had not been, for some time, all that a fond father could wish. She was uncertain of temper, she had headaches, she had fits of gloom, quite unlike the usual even tenor of her shallow way. When Norah came she improved. For Ella fancied herself in love, and chose to assume injured airs because her father still spoke of Frank Perrymont.

She was in love with Jack Armstrong, though Jack had never addressed his attentions to her in any way, as Mr. Bayliss, who was acute enough to see the reason of these humours, very well knew. At the same time he was not displeased. It came more and more into his mind that Jack was the man who would carry on the works, while Frank Perrymont would let things slide. Perhaps, too, there was a secret, half-acknowledged thought of retribution due.

There were other complications. Frank Perrymont, who ought to have fallen in love, as was arranged by both parents, with Ella Bayliss, chose to think himself in love with Norah. At the croquet parties, at the little dances, at after-dinner musical evenings, it was with Norah that he tried to get up a flirtation. As a noticeable point, Frank was always in love. With Ella Bayliss as a central figure, at which he was destined some time or other to settle, he hovered like a butterfly from flower to flower. Norah attracted him more than any girl he had ever met.

"It is not her beauty," he said, "though

she is as beautiful as a dark-eyed Venus of the Isles, and as straight as Diana, but it is her voice that I love. They say that a soft voice is a sweet thing in women. Nonsense! I hate your soft voices. I like a musical voice. Norah's voice is as full of poetry as a page of Tennyson. It whispers and sings all sorts of impossible delights. When I hear it, I am carried away to some earthly Paradise where it is always afternoon. I come away from her filled with strange thoughts. Ella Bayliss is a beautiful girl, but Norah Cuolahan is more than beautiful. She is a muse. She would do for Alfred de Musset's invisible form which cheers and sustains the drooping poet."

He wrote verses for her; openly, for airs which he raked out of old portfolios: secretly, poems which he kept in his desk, or sometimes showed to her. Norah accepted the homage not with any sense of what was meant, but with the proud air of a woman who takes whatever gifts men offer her as a natural tribute. It is the prerogative of a goddess to make no sign when the votive offering is laid upon her shrine.

"Norah," said Ella, "'I see something. Frank Perrymont is in love."

"With you, dear?" said Norah calmly.

"No, not with me at all, though papa is so eager for it. He is in love with quite somebody else."

"You mean me?" asked Norah calmly. "My dear Ella, men never know what they mean, to begin with; and if they do, they always mean the wrong thing. At any rate, I am not in love with Mr. Perrymont. And I think it extremely bad taste in him to act so as to make you think him faithless in his allegiance."

Then Ella pouted, and was silent for an hour. But she said no more about Frank Perrymont.

One day, the young man sought his father in his laboratory. Here, surrounded by the shades of Cornelius Agrippa, Albertus Magnus, Jean de Meung, and other great alchemists, and amid a thousand glass bottles and retorts, the enthusiast pursued the silent studies which would lead him to the discovery of the elixir vitæ, or at least the philosopher's stone.

"I want to speak to you, father," said the young man, "about myself. Can you give me five minutes?"

"Yes, if you can wait ten."

He was conducting an experiment with a crucible. Like the rest of the alchemists, the Captain was always discovering something new in chemistry. To be sure, he never hit on any new discovery that was not already known to the world, but that mattered nothing. He made a note of it in the big books about which his will had made ample provision, and went on calmly. It was just as if any one were to rediscover, in their latter days, the force of gravity, the laws of attraction, or the Copernican system, and then, after making solemn note of his find, to issue rigid instructions about giving it to the world after his death. The Captain, had he found the elixir vitæ, would probably have abstained from drinking any himself, because he was a religious man; but would have left his secret behind him, as his predecessors did, wrapped in an obscure enigma.

"Now, Frank, what is it?"

"I am in love, sir," said Frank, with an ingenuous blush.

"Yes? It is a phenomenon natural at your age. Let me see. I was thirty when I fell in love with your mother, the best of women, and married her. You are five and twenty, I suppose. Yes, it is natural. I hope it is with the right girl, Frank."

"It is with Norah Cuolahan, the best of all good girls."

"Norah Cuolahan!" said the Captain. "The daughter of an Irish rent collector, made a lady by education. I was in hopes you were going to say it was with Ella Bayliss."

"The daughter of an uneducated scrap-factory owner, who made himself rich by good luck, and made his daughter a lady by education," retorted Frank.

"*Habet*," returned his father, laughing. "A fair parry, Frank. But Bayliss and I have many things in common. We are both made rich by good luck. Before the iron turned up, I had five hundred a year and this house, and nothing else. Now, if you marry Ella Bayliss——"

"But I love Norah Cuolahan."

"Does she love you? You see, love is a double-barrelled kind of weapon."

"'Il y a toujours un qui aime et un qui est aimé,'" said Frank.

"Don't throw your immoral French proverbs at me, sir," said his father. "Your mother and I loved each other, and the result was——"

"Well, sir?".

"Well, sir," said the Captain, rubbing his nose, "one of the results was yourself. Another was that your poor mother was a happy woman. A third, if less consideration, was that I was a happy man. Now, Frank, there is no talking, between us, of ways and means. You shall marry where you please, provided that I am certain beforehand that the young lady loves you for yourself. Any girl in Esbrough would jump at your income. I don't want a jumping Jenny for you. Show me a girl who loves you, as your mother loved me, and you shall have her."

"May I speak to Norah?" asked Frank.

The Captain sat down and meditated.

"Before I proposed," he said, "I found out that your mother loved me. I was suspicious, so I watched her with other young fellows. I was only a lieutenant then, on leave. I flirted with girls—ugly girls, you know, so as not to create any diversion in my own feelings; for the passion of love is as uncertain as the weather in the Channel, and before you know where you are, you are blown on quite another tack."

"I suppose ugly girls have their feelings, sir," said Frank. "If you pinch them, they squeal; if you tickle them, they laugh; if you prick them, they bleed; if you make love to them and mean nothing, they suffer."

"The boy's right," said the Captain. "Gad, Frank! I believe I've been a great sinner!"

Then he chuckled, as all men do after fifty, at the recollection of their sins; men under fifty like to be considered gay young rovers still. Their wives humour them, and pretend to be jealous.

"Well, sir, I tried my wife: before I married her I discovered that she cared nothing about anybody else; that she was jealous if I flirted; and that she had fixed her heart on me. So I gave her myself; and we even had a poor half-dozen years of happiness. Then she died, poor thing!—poor thing!" The Captain cleared his throat, and went on: "Now bring your Norah Cuolahan here, and I will subject her to experiments. Then I will tell you.

I have watched her—a mighty pretty girl! with her black eyes—soft black eyes, too, not great staring black eyes—and her pretty head! I am not so blind as most men of my age!"

"You are an old sailor, sir," said the diplomate, his son.

"True, Frank, true; there's nobody so wise as an old salt. Her voice, too!"

"Did you ever hear her sing, sir?"

"Am I deaf?" he replied, with huge contempt. "Singing?—I have actually found the tears come into my eyes when she sang an Irish ballad."

"Did you ever see her own eyes swimming with tears while she was singing?"

"I like her lips, Frank; her ripe, rosy lips, like a rose-bud! Gad, sir! I always think of Henri Quatre and the young lady who was going to be a nun: 'Who is your father, my pretty dear?' asked the jolly king. 'I am the daughter of God, sire,' said the girl. 'Ventre Saint Gris!' said the king; 'I'd like to be his son-in-law!' Norah Cuolahan is a saint when she sings; she's an angel when she sits silent; she's a woman. Eh, sir?"— the Captain began to walk up and down the room—"she will be a woman when she puts her arms round some lucky devil's neck, and says, 'I love you!' Frank, you dog! if you get Norah, you'll be the luckiest man alive! But no tampering with her affections. Wait till I make my experiments upon her."

"Upon my word, sir," said Frank, "I believe you are in love with her yourself!"

CHAPTER XII.

The Captain, left alone, sat down and began to think.

Was he in love with Norah Cuolahan? At his age—at fifty-five—to fall in love with a girl of eighteen? It was so absurd that he began to laugh, but choked. And then he turned fiery red, for he thought of certain passages that had passed between himself and another lady—older, it was true, than Norah, but still—but still—— He contrasted the two.

"Pshaw!" he cried, pacing the floor of his laboratory, "what can an old fool like me expect but painted cheeks and artificial ways? Of course, Adelaide paints, and she's full of airs; but she's a lady—widow of a general officer, too. And little Norah is the daughter of a collector of rents;—a man you could not ask to dinner. And yet, what would it matter? The little witch!—the soft-eyed little witch! What a devil of a thing it is to get old! We ought to have three lives at least; and a beautiful woman in every one."

Then he broke off the subject in his mind, and resumed the current of his thoughts, set steadily, with few interruptions, in the direction of the elixir vitæ and the philosopher's stone.

But he did not forget his promised experiments.

Mrs. Merrion came home again, and in a temper which boded storm. Something had happened. Outwardly, she was calm; but Mrs. Bastable's experience warned her that the most tranquil weather frequently precedes a hurricane of the most violent kind. Pauline privately imparted to Mrs. Bastable the fact that the glass had been fixed at "set stormy" for some days past, ever since the receipt of a letter. Keziah was not a brave woman, but she was not afraid of Mrs. Merrion; and at the worst times, when Pauline would run shuddering like a vessel with close-reefed sails before a gale, and when the housemaid would burst into tears of trembling fear, beneath the cascade of invective which dropped, instead of pearls, from this angry lady's lips, Keziah would calmly front the danger, and reduce her to silence by mere indifference of the nervous system. A woman in wrath, you see, is like a woman in love: she requires sympathy, support, and reciprocity. Now, Keziah afforded none of these aids; so that Mrs. Merrion, when Pauline was routed and the housemaid reduced to rags, ran down of her own accord.

On this occasion, when she was quite spent, Mrs. Bastable asked quietly what the matter was.

"You go up to London in a temper, Jenny," she said, "and you come back in a temper; and I'm sure I don't know why."

"And I'm not going to tell you," answered her cousin. "I suppose I can be in a temper if I like. I'm my own mistress."

Then she sat down and wrote a letter.

"My own Jack," it began. "I received your note, which was sent on to London to me, and was astonished at the contents. You may, if you please, refuse to keep to your written word. All the same, I have it, and shall make what use I please of it. And my first use will be to go to Mr. Fortescue with it, and show it to him. He will be able to form his own judgment about the character for honour, truth, and constancy which you will deserve.

"But I am not writing to threaten you. I refuse to accept your letter. I appeal to the long evenings we have passed together, to the words you have spoken, to the kisses which I feel on my cheek always, for I never loved anybody, really, except you, and until I am your wife I shall always be your betrothed.
—ADELAIDE."

Looking for an envelope in her writing-table, she came upon two or three other documents, which she read with a curious smile.

"I am a great fool," she said to herself. "I am infatuated with this boy, who will get tired of me in a week and make my life miserable for me in a month. Let him take care. If he does I can make his more miserable, if I tell him all. I am indeed a fool. What is the boy, after all? Oh, Jack! if I could get your brown curls out of my heart, I might be Mrs. Perrymont, or Mrs. Bayliss—Queen of Esbrough — to-morrow, for here are their letters to say so. But I can't—I can't. I think always of the time when he threw his arms—his great strong arms—round my neck, and told me he loved me. Good honest love it was then, such love as few women get; the first and best, and the most constant, if it is properly handled. And I think he did love me once, or was it only a kind of intoxication? Men used to tell me, in the old days, that I intoxicated them with my eyes. I am getting old now, but my eyes remain the same. I must have bewitched him as I used to bewitch all the rest. I *will* marry him—I will. I will have neither the stiff-necked old Captain with his chemicals, nor the red-faced Bayliss, fifty-five if he's a day, with his pompous self-conceit. I will have my Jack, my handsome, my bonny Jack. And as for that Norah girl, I wish I could poison her."

She looked as if she could for a moment, then she laughed in her hollow way.

"Norah? The girl is a lady, and I am only

half a lady. Well, but then I know the world. She is nineteen and I am turned five and thirty. But then I know things and she knows nothing. Bah! she is a chit. And here I have Jack's letters. And if the worst comes to the worst, I will bring an action against him. I am the widow of General Merrion of the Confederate Service, formerly of Louisiana. Who is to say I am not? I defy them to prove a single thing, or even to bring forward a single charge. Here are his letters. 'Dearest Adelaide,' 'Dearest,' 'My own,' all written on bits of note-paper and sent across the street in answer to mine. Jack, my boy, I've got you under my thumb. You are mine, and nobody else's. Pretty Norah! Poor little child. I shall see your insolent contemptuous cheeks grow pale, my dear. I shall see the light in your eyes grow dim. I shall watch you pining away, when you know that he is to be married, and married to ME. For you love him; I saw you flush when I said you were his sister. You love him; and for all your demurity, sleekness, and purity, Countess of Connaught, you shall sorrow and be miserable." Then she laughed again. And then she stopped, put up the letters and took a hasty look at herself in the chimney-glass, for she heard the knock of a visitor. "Who is that?" she said. "Is it Paul Bayliss? I do hope not. He is too insufferable. Or is it Captain Perrymont? Or is it Myles Cuolahan? I hope it is Myles. He is the one who admires me most. But it can't be him. He only comes when his daughter is out."

It was no other than Captain Perrymont, who entered in his quiet and thoughtful way, and sat down.

"So you've come back, Mrs. Merrion."

"I have come back, Captain Perrymont."

"Ah! Yes. You're looking very well to-night—a—a—Adelaide."

The Captain had been a sailor, you see. And a pretty woman has always charms to a sailor. Besides, he was going to do what he thought was a cruel thing.

"Thank you," she said, shifting her chair a little nearer his. "Thank you. Yes. I am very well indeed. What is the matter with you, this evening?"

For Captain Perrymont, sooth to say, had

been wont to show more ardour in his visits at the beginning of an interview, though he sometimes slacked off towards the finish.

"Well, Adelaide," he began, refreshing himself with a kiss, "I can't help it, and couldn't if I was eighty, instead of fifty-four and three-quarters. The fact is, I've been thinking that a certain letter I sent you was a mistake."

"I've got six letters from you," she replied, "all kept, and all locked up. Which is the mistaken letter?"

The Captain changed colour. But he remembered that he had once been in command of a frigate, and encouraged himself.

"They are all mistaken. I want them back."

"Captain Perrymont asks me to marry him," said Mrs. Merrion softly, addressing the world in general. "He takes advantage of my promise to kiss me, and the next minute he says it was all a mistake."

"Kissing you!" murmured the Captain. "Now, I put it to you, my dear—did ever a man find himself in your company alone for an hour without doing the same thing?"

She laughed. Some ladies would have taken it for an insult. Mrs. Merrion received it as a compliment to her beauty. Nevertheless, she disclaimed it.

"I suppose you think that I allow all the world to make love to me. You are mistaken again, Captain Perrymont. But see. You want me to give up your letters. What if I refuse?"

"Then I offer to buy them back."

"That is frank," she replied.

"I like to call things by their right names. You made a fool of me, and I am not going to marry you. You have letters by which you can make a fool of me in the public courts, if you like. A woman looks a greater fool, however. Now will you give me my letters back?"

"Captain Perrymont"—Mrs. Merrion turned upon him quickly—"you are in love with another woman. Lord, man, don't look ashamed. There is many another old fool in the world. You are in love, and it is no use trying to hide it, with Norah Cuolahan."

The Captain answered nothing.

"So is your son. But Norah will never love him."

"Will she not? Why not? How do you know?"

"Oh! I know many things. Norah will not marry your son: whether she will marry your son's father is quite another question. She is poor; you are rich: she has no position; you are a gentleman: she is without any prospects; you will assure her future. Upon my word, Captain Perrymont, I think you have a very good chance. Now, look here. You are wrong in supposing that I will sell your letters to you, at least, for the present. I will do nothing of the kind. To begin with, I am not altogether destitute, as you know. I have enough for a woman's simple wants"—including champagne, Chateau Lafitte, and curaçoa, which were among her simple wants. "I am not a mercenary woman. When you told me you loved me" —she drew out a pocket-handkerchief to conceal the dryness of her eyes—"when you said you loved me, I thought myself a happy woman at last. My poor dear general was a good man, but he was too old, and full of ailments. I was his nurse. I thought that the time had come when, no longer a young woman—I am already past eight-and-twenty—I was to have a husband; one to whom I could look for protection as well as love. But it is not to be. Sir, Captain Perrymont, I can be generous. On the day when you tell me that Norah Cuolahan is engaged to you, I give you back your letters. But not before. And now, sir, good night. Trifle with no other woman's happiness. Go, Captain Perrymont! Go! and forget your—your—p-p-poor, poor Adelaide."

She fell back on the sofa in an ecstasy of tears, her face buried in her hands. The Captain, preserving his equanimity under these trying circumstances, saw on the desk his own bundle of letters. Noiselessly and rapidly he possessed himself of them, and slid them into his pocket. It was done in a moment. Then he began to soothe her.

"My poor Adelaide," he said. "I am grieved indeed that my hasty words could hurt your feelings. Had I known, before, that you were touched by the supposed affections of an old boy like me, I should have acted differently. You are a very generous woman, by Gad; and—and—" here his voice choked, for he thought of the letters in his pocket, and he was on the point of a chuckle, but refrained in time. "Good-bye, Adelaide. Let an old fellow have one more kiss."

She turned half a cheek to him, a very fair cheek, and the gallant Captain impressed a fervent kiss upon it. Then he disappeared, walking down the road, with an occasional tap of his pocket to ascertain the existence of the letters.

"Well out of that, old salt," he said, shaking his head; "deuced well out of that! She's a pirate, or I'm mistaken. And to think of her finding me out. There's Cuolahan's cottage, and there—hang me, if there isn't Frank in the garden!"

It was a bright moonlight night in August, about half-past ten. The Captain stood under a tree in the shade. The front of the cottage was lit up by the white moonlight. A single window, on the first floor, was lit up. In the garden sat Myles, with his pipe in his mouth, while Frank was tootling on the flute.

"It's lovely, Mr. Frank," said Myles; "lovely. When I was a boy at Ennis, where the fair was—you'll have heard of Ennis fair—

there was a boy about your weight, though I think he'd have doubled you up with a shillalah, used to handle a flute as I'd handle a knife and fork. They bruk his head once over a wake they had—it was my own father's first cousin twice removed—and after that, divil a chune he'd play but " Croppies, lie down " : and so, poor fellow, he got his head bruk so often, that once he laid down and never got up again. Kilt entirely, he was."

Frank was thinking of Norah, and began to play something else.

" The puppy's serenading her, I believe."

When the air was half finished, Norah's head came out of the window.

" No, Mr. Perrymont! " she said sweetly; " my father has to get up early in the morning; and I have to get up to give him his breakfast. So you will not keep him out any longer, I am sure."

Frank pulled his flute to pieces, shook hands with Myles, and quickly walked away.

" Ho! ho! " said his father. " Ho! ho! and about this time Adelaide has found out about the letters. Here's a good night's work."

Adelaide had not, however, found out about the letters. She swept all together, Jack's and the rest, into a drawer, as soon as her visitor had gone, and then rung the bell for Mrs. Bastable.

"Now, Keziah," she said, in great good-humour, for the prospect of Norah's possible advance in life afforded her every gratification. "Now, Keziah, my dear, get the brandy and water, and give me my cigarettes, and let us have a talk. Tell me all about the stupid Esbrough people. Has the curate person called? He's but a poor pump, but he has the good taste to admire me. I wept over his last sermon, right under his silly nose. If that lawyer's wife calls, I had best be civil to her: lawyers are always to be cultivated. For I am going to change my life, Keziah—not too much water—and I am going into society a little more. That's right! Now mix for yourself, my good soul, and talk to me."

She really was, as she said herself, only half a lady.

"Some people would call this ungentlemanly, I am afraid," said the Captain, burning the letters one by one in the candle. "But, Lord! what does it matter? A pretty fool I should have looked in a witness-box for a breach of promise. 'Is this your writing, sir? Don't equivocate. Answer me, yes or no?' 'It certainly is, my Lord.' 'Read it, Mr. Pumphandle.' 'My dearest Adelaide, I have been thinking over you all the night, so that I hardly had more than eight hours' sleep. When shall I call you mine?' Toorul-loo! 'When shall I call you my own for ever?' Ho! ho! ho! what a rage she will be in!"

Captain Perrymont next proceeded to make his promised experiments upon Norah. He gave an afternoon party, one of those much affected in the neighbourhood, where a luncheon at four allowed the abolition of dinner and dress, and supper afterwards. It was a strange old house, that of the Perrymonts'. A tower, like one of the Peels of Northumberland, once a little fortress near the coast, had tacked on to one side of it a small Elizabethan house, with diamond lattices, tall gables, and much wood carving. This was now the servants' quarters. On the other side was a stately house, warm, comfortable, and ugly, of Queen Anne's date, practically belonging to Frank Perrymont, because the Captain lived in the tower. In front was a lawn, and round the house stood what was called the park, but it was of small dimensions, though planted with trees and laid out to the best advantage. It was five miles from Esbrough, and the Captain's works were to be seen, when the wind blew from the west so as to drive the smoke in the opposite direction, plainly in the distance. And it gave him no pain that next to his works stood those of Mr. Bayliss, bigger than his own, and belonging to a richer man.

He detached Miss Ferens from the croquet players, and led her for a walk about the grounds, talking of Norah.

"She is a prize for a duke, my dear Miss Ferens," he said in his grandest manner. "There is no man who ought not to be proud in marrying Miss Cuolahan—Norah, I may call her, to you."

"She has not the accident of birth," said Miss Ferens, "but she has everything else."

"Not fortune, my dear lady."

THIS SON OF VULCAN. 65

"She will have all that I have. It is not a great fortune, but it is something."

"I wish I was five and twenty. It is hard upon us old fellows, Miss Ferens, to see these angels of beauty, and feel that they are out of your reach."

"Captain Perrymont, you have married once, and you have had your share of youth and beauty. Be content. Besides, it is absurd that a man cannot see a pretty girl without talking nonsense about her. It would make you no happier if you could take Norah in your arms and kiss her at once."

The Captain gave her a funny look. Make him no happier to take the girl in his arms and kiss and cuddle her? Good heavens! to think of the senseless nature of elderly womankind.

After luncheon, at which he did the honours in the most stately style, for he was proud of being at the head of his own table, and that a well-appointed one, he left the rest of his guests to stroll about, and attached himself to Norah. Frank, disappointed, began to turn over music with Ella Bayliss.

"Play something, Frank," said his father.

"My son plays the flute with remarkable sweetness, Miss Cuolahan—very remarkable sweetness. Did you ever hear him?"

Frank, bending over the portfolio, blushed, but no one saw him.

"Oh yes!" said Norah, in her frank way. "I heard him the other night. He was spending the evening with my father, and played to us."

Ella looked up, radiant. Frank, then, was in love with Norah.

"Come, Miss Cuolahan," said the Captain, "and I will show you my den, where I work."

He led her to the tower. On the first floor, raised by a dozen steps from the ground, was his own bedroom, a camp bed standing in the corner, and rows of books round the walls. That was all the furniture, save a sword hung above the bed, and the model of a ship.

"My sword," said the Captain. "It hasn't seen much fighting, but it has seen some. I left the service before the Crimean War. Here is a model of my last ship. Ah! she was a beauty of the old school. Look at her lines. Look at her rig. Look at her stern.

And to think that ironclads have come into fashion. My dear young lady, though I am a man of science, I am also a sailor, and it is enough to break a man's heart. Come upstairs."

Up a stair so steep as to be almost a ladder, the Captain conducted his guest. She found herself, at the top, in a circular room round which shelves ran, laden with countless bottles. A few books lay on the table in the centre. Where should have been the fireplace was a furnace. Curious diagrams lay about on chairs, marked with figures in black and red, signs which might mean anything.

"You are looking at my horoscopes," said the Captain.

"What are horoscopes?"

"They are calculations, founded on an ancient science as old as the Chaldeans, of which I am almost the only scholar left in England. This is my own. I calculated it a few years ago. It contains a prognostication of my wife's early death and my own great good fortune."

"But your wife died, and your fortune came

before the prognostication was made. Is that prophesying, Captain Perrymont?"

"What does it matter, if the nativity comes true, when it is calculated?" returned the astrologer. "Well now, Miss Cuolahan, here is your own nativity. I only calculated that a few days ago. You are nineteen. You have all your life before you. Shall I read it to you?"

"If it is a lucky life," said Norah, hesitating.

"I am glad that you are not afraid. It is here. I find that you were born on the——"

"You were told all that. Pass on to the future."

"You will marry. You will be happy. I am not quite certain whom you will marry. Something seems to interfere."

"If I am to be happy," murmured the girl, "I know whom I shall marry."

Captain Perrymont took his eye-glasses off his nose and laid down the document.

"Is Miss Cuolahan engaged?" he asked.

"No, sir," said Norah. "And you have no right to ask the question."

"Pardon me. I have not," he returned. "Only, I am a man a great deal older than you, my dear young lady, and I took the privilege of my years. Pray forgive me."

"I forgive you," she said, smiling.

"Is—let me ask a question or two. It is not mere idle curiosity. Is—is——" The Captain's power of making experiments seemed to be eclipsed for the moment, for he stammered painfully. "Miss Cuolahan, I have observed a certain leaning towards you on the part of a—a young man—an extremely young man, in whom I take an interest."

"I cannot answer enigmas," said Norah.

"He is a rich young man, the son of a rich man."

"Oh! then it isn't——" interrupted the girl, ungrammatically.

"In fact," said the Captain, growing desperate, "it is my own son, Frank."

"Captain Perrymont, did your son ask you to speak to me?"

"No, that is—you see—I know."

"Then, if he did not, I can answer you. It is impossible, absolutely impossible, that I could ever listen to your son. Do not mistake me. I like him very much. He is very nice, and I am sure he is good. But I could not, oh! I could not *think* of marrying him."

The Captain's face beamed with satisfaction.

"I always thought that Frank was a jackanapes," he said. "He is too young, is he not?"

"Much too young," said Norah, in great confusion, and hardly knowing what she said.

"What you want," pursued Captain Perrymont, "is an older, a steadier man—eh? one whose habits are fixed; a man of good position: perhaps a little elderly."

"Oh! I don't know what I want," said Norah impatiently. "I want nothing."

"Miss Cuolahan," he began again, in a solemn voice.

"I shall go downstairs, I think, and join the others," said Norah quickly.

"One moment, pray—only one moment. Miss Cuolahan—Norah, if the love of Frank's father can make you happy, take it and be his wife."

Norah looked him straight in the face. She neither laughed, nor cried, nor blushed.

"I take it very kindly of you, Captain Perrymont. You have an interest in me, and you think I am unprotected and friendless. That is not so, indeed. I am not afraid for myself. As I cannot marry your son, you think I might marry you, just to assure me a home. It is good of you; but of course I can only say that I thank you—and—and——"

The Captain recovered himself at once. Without the least apparent emotion, he opened his arms upon the air as if to get rid of an unpleasant subject.

"You refuse, Miss Cuolahan. Well—it is not quite what you think. I persuaded myself that I loved you. I believe I do, too, but I shall see after a while. You are so pretty and so clever, and so different from the girls one meets, that really I think there is some excuse for the folly of an old boy like me. Shake hands, my dear, and don't tell Frank, or anybody else. Well, well. That is finished. Of course I can't have two lives, any more than other people, till I've finished my work here. Then, indeed—would perennial youth and boundless wealth tempt you, child? Should you like to keep your health and beauty and to have everything that gold can procure for you? That is what I can offer you, but not yet, not yet."

"That is your dream, Captain Perrymont. Are you going to make gold out of those pots and pans?"

"My dream indeed. And as yet I seem only on the threshold. See. Here are all the books ever written—that I could hear of —on the subject. This old French poet gives the secret in a ballad, but I am too thick to understand. Cornelius gives the secret in an enigma, but I cannot read it. Albertus tells it a dozen times over in his books to those who have been initiated. I have searched everywhere for the Rosicrucians, but it is no use. I have gone to spirit-compellers, but their utterances have helped me in no way. Love, indeed, for me? Why, my dear girl, I spend the whole day and half the night in this tower. Some day I shall die here. What an ass I am! What an ass I am, to be sure! And so you can't marry Frank, eh? Well, what must he do? Go away, to cure himself?"

"Not at all. I will cure him. And he must marry Ella Bayliss. Think how rich you will be, then; and you can lock up the laboratory door and go outside among the flowers for the rest of your life."

"Go, girl," said the Captain, in good temper. "Go—you have no mind for science. Give me a kiss, you wilful queen, and be very glad you said no to an old donkey."

CHAPTER XIII.

Miss Ferens could hardly understand the difference that a few months had made in Norah. The girl, who was only a girl, had become a woman: all her fun and frolic had gone out of her: she was grave, staid, sober. Life was serious for her, since the day when Jack had spoken. It is so with women: love awakens love: what was before only a vague inclination, an unsatisfied unknown desire, an incomprehensible restlessness, becomes a fierce flame of passion, when the man has told what is in his heart: and not before. Girls do not fall in love: they have preferences: they think one man better than another: but not until the man they "fancy," to use the homely phrase, comes, do they permit the full current of love to flow through their veins. Love springs full born in the brain of a man, like Athéné in the brain of Zeus : love, a tiny infant at first, in the heart of a woman, stretches out vague hands here and there, catching feebly at unknown distances, till the magician, Speech, gives it knowledge, power, and ripeness. Norah was in love, because Jack had spoken. She had loved him always, she said; but what was her love when Jack was a sort of brother, compared to that which now filled all her heart, and made life a sweet, intelligible, serious whole? Then she had learned more of the world. In Esbrough the grades of a society essentially bourgeois amused and interested her. Unlike that quiet Bedesbury aisle, where a few cathedral dignitaries made all the set, the Esbrough people had their fierce jealousies and bickerings. And they looked with jealousy amounting to a divine wrath on the girl whose father was nothing, positively lower than nothing, on whom they could not afford to call, going everywhere, and into the best.

About this time, too, Myles became restless. If you put the Bedouin Arab into a town, he lies about for a few days, happy in the change; but if you keep him too long, he begins to pine for the fresh free air of the desert. Myles had been a wanderer and an Arab for a good many years. While Jack was with him, he was content to be a dweller among houses,—was proud, too, of a newly-gained respectability; but when Jack was gone, there was nobody, not even his daughter, to whom he could pour out his soul. Norah taught him: in every action, in every gesture, in every word, he recognised in the girl the existence of a world of thought, on whose threshold he was standing, with a sort of wonder and curiosity. He learned many things from her, but he could not talk to her. Between her and himself there seemed to be some hedge, too tall for him to look over. And if he tried to open his heart, it was timidly, and with a fear that he should say something that would make her ashamed of him. This was Myles's great terror, that she should be ashamed of him. Then came Miss Ferens, in whose presence he was constrained and stiff, because she knew the dreadful past.

"Don't tell her, Miss Ferens, ma'am," he whispered in an agitated voice. "Don't tell her."

She knew what he meant, and renewed her promise. And then there came upon him, like a wave, the desire to be once more upon the road, if only for a week. He grew restless: he prowled about the house after dark, instead of sitting at home, as he had been wont to do.

"I can't help it, alaunah," he said one night, when Norah came out and found him marching backwards and forwards in the road. "I can't help it; but the desire's strong upon me to go back to the old life."

"Not, and leave me, father?"

"That's it, my darlin', that's what keeps me here. I can't leave you. It's ungrateful to think of it. It's a cruel wrong I'd do you. But I can't sleep at night; and all day long I think of the green fields, and the road, and the evenings, and the story-tellin', and—oh! Norah, my angel, that's sent by the blessed Lord to bring me to heaven, I'm sickening to see them all again."

"Then why not go, father? You can get a holiday for a month. Leave Miss Ferens to take care of me, and go."

He gasped at the chance, and thinking,

when he went to bed, of the old life to begin again, slept soundly.

Something happened which kept him in Esbrough for a while. For one morning, while Miss Ferens and Norah were sitting at work in Norah's room, there came along the road a miserable old man. A disgraceful old man; an old man all in rags, dirt, and tatters; a mumbling old man, one who shook his head from side to side, and had protruding lips that trembled when he talked to himself; an old man with flowing white hair. After him followed a tail of boys, hooting and cheering. And at sight of that horrible old man Norah rushed out of the room, and before Miss Ferens had recovered her surprise, had him into the house, and on a chair, still feebly murmuring and muttering.

"Hush, dear," she said. "Don't say anything. Only get me some milk, if there is any. It is the best thing for him."

Miss Ferens got a cup of milk, which the poor old creature swallowed eagerly, and then looked about the room.

"It's a man named Cardiff," Norah whispered. "It is he who tried to murder Jack. He is old and half mad."

"Cardiff's my name," he bawled out loud. "And I'm not ashamed of it. Captain Cardiff, General Cardiff, Gentleman Cardiff, Prince of all the road—Cardiff's my name."

Then his voice dropped suddenly to a whisper.

"He's after me, Miss Norah—he's after me again: all the same as when I came here last. Oh! I remember—when you gave me food and drink . . . ah! it's years ago . . . years ago . . . years ago. He's after me again."

"He's dangerous, dear," whispered Miss Ferens. "What can we do for him? Can't you persuade him to go?"

"Not yet, dear. Wait a little."

"He's after me, Miss Norah—the boy I murdered. I can't keep away from Esbrough. And I came back to see the place, and I can't find it. You know all about it: you know everything. I tied him hard and fast, the pretty boy, to the ribs of the old barge, and the tide came up, and came up, and came up —and he never cried and never asked for mercy: and I drank up all the rum in the bottle, and went to sleep and forgot him. And when I awoke in the morning it was broad daylight, and the tide was gone out and the wreck too—and he was drowned. I murdered him. And I want to see the place where I did it. And I can't find it—I can't find it. . . . The boys throw stones at me. They call me names. If they knew they would kill me too. Don't tell them!" he cried, in an ecstasy of terror. "Don't tell them, Miss Norah, or they'll murder me too. And I'm too young to die—because I haven't repented yet. If I could find the place where I did it, I should be able to repent. But I can't. It isn't there: they've taken it away; and somehow I can't rightly remember."

"Suppose," said Norah, "that he wasn't dead, after all?"

"Don't talked damned nonsense!" he answered in a rough voice, "because I did it, I tell you. Some time ago, I saw somebody like him—I don't know where: I think it was somewhere near you, Miss Norah. I remember your name. Oh yes! . . . . Ha! ha! ha! I remember you. You gave me cold mutton, and then I thought I would rob you of your purse—and did it. Ha! ha! Cardiff Jack must keep up his reputation."

It is a curious psychological fact that he forgot the crimes he had actually committed, and remembered only those he had intended to commit.

"There was a young fellow like little Jack Armstrong, only big and strong. I hated him. I got the men to kill him with stones. Serve him right. But I wish I hadn't murdered the poor little boy. Because I can't get away from him. He drives me always back here. And it's through him that I can't think. And it's him that's brought me to trouble. I've had nothing but trouble ever since I murdered him. That was a bad day, Gentleman Cardiff, that was a bad day."

He went on maundering, the two women looking on helplessly. Presently he stopped, and, dropping his head between his hands, fell fast asleep.

"What on earth shall we do, Norah?"

"We must send for the doctor, dear, and get a nurse."

They did so, the man slumbering tranquilly.

In the afternoon the nurse and the doctor came. They undressed the poor old creature, washed him, and put him to bed. When

Myles came home, Norah told him of his guest. He at once proposed that Mr. Cardiff should be transferred to the curbstone, to lie there till he died.

" 'Tis he," he cried, " that nearly murdered Jack. Norah, have you got no love for poor Jack, that you'll harbour his murderer? 'Tis he that I thrashed. Look—here's the cut I got against his teeth. I told Mr. Fortescue that I would forgive him, when I'd hammered him, and not till then. 'Tis he that drove Jack out of the works and away among the foreigners; and Lord knows when I'll see him again. Norah, I didn't think it of you—you, that should have turned upon him and driven him down the road with the boys throwin' stones, and the men duckin' him in the horse-pond; you, that should have laughed at every misfortune."

" Father ! " Norah cried hoarsely, " remember what you said last night."

" What did I say, alaunah ? "

" You said, dear, that God had sent me to bring you to heaven. God help us both, if that is the way I have done my duty."

" What is it at all, my daughter ? "

"Father, forgive us our sins, as we forgive those that sin against us and against the ones we love," said the girl.

Myles was silent for a while.

"I can't, Norah, my sunshine. I can't. I'd try to, but I can't. When I think of the night I wandered about the shore looking for Jack, crying for Jack, and found him in the boat in the morning more dead than alive—I can't, Norah. But have it your own way. Only don't ask me yet. For I am not able to do it. Let me see him."

He was lying asleep, as peacefully as a child, this robber and murderer. Sleep had smoothed out the lines of his face: his mouth was pursed in a gentle smile.

"Look at him," murmured Myles. "Only to look at him, Miss Ferens, that's the biggest rogue in all England. He's the king of rogues. There's nobody to touch him. I knew him well, once."

"Mr. Cuolahan," returned Miss Ferens, "do not recall too much."

Myles collapsed, and suffered himself to be led away.

In the middle of the night Norah was

awakened by a cautious step. She wrapped a dressing-gown round her and hurried out. As she suspected, Mr. Cardiff, in the only robe they had left him with, was slowly creeping down the stairs. He carried a candle. She followed him. He went first into Jack's room, which was pitch-dark. Then he came out, armed with a long chisel, the first thing he came across, and made for the kitchen. Norah followed him still, with a stiffening of her nerves. He placed the candle on the table and began to hunt about the room. Norah stepped towards him, and caught him by the arm.

"What do you want, Mr. Cardiff?"

"Drink!" he replied; "drink! Give me drink. I will have it!"

"There is water," she said, pouring him out a glass from a jug. "Drink that."

"Put some rum in it. Put some rum in it. I will have it. I know who you are. You are Miss Norah. I know well. I forget how I know. It's night, and there's no one else in the house. Give me rum, or I will kill you."

"You will not kill me," replied the girl,

looking him full in the face. "And I will not give you any spirits. Go to bed, Mr. Cardiff, and be ashamed of yourself."

"I must have drink. Give me beer, give me whisky, give me rum, give me anything. I must have it. Drink makes me young: drink makes me forget: drink makes me remember: drink makes me happy. Give me drink, I say."

"You had best not raise your voice," said Norah, "or you will wake my father."

"The nurse is asleep," he went on, chuckling to himself. "I've been in hospitals, and I know a nurse when I see her. She's asleep, and here I am. Now then, I'm not afraid of you. Give me the drink, before I get desperate."

"Mr. Cardiff," she replied, "you are an old man. Think how you murdered the little boy—the poor little boy."

"I want to forget it. Where is the bottle?"

"You cannot forget it. Every day he follows you: every night you hear his voice at your bedside: you see his eyes in the darkness."

He groaned, and dropped the chisel.

Norah adroitly put her foot on it, and drew it under the folds of her dress.

"You have that crime upon your mind. The time will come when you will be laid upon a sick-bed, unable to move. You will have no drink there: you will be unable to escape the voice of conscience: you will be ill, weak, and dying. And that boy's murder will be heavier than any lead. And there will be no one to help you."

He stood shivering in every limb.

"And you want to bring another murder upon your head. Wretched man! is not one enough?"

"It is too much. Oh! for mercy's sake, help me to forget."

"I will. Kneel down with me, and say what I say."

They knelt—this poor old hardened tramp, on whose conscience every conceivable crime lay like a leaden cowl, and the fresh, innocent girl, who knew nothing of sin but what she had read. They knelt, and the old villain, whose mind was weak and wandering, seemed to remember something about the talisman of virtue and innocence, for he followed in a low voice, and word for word, while she pleaded for mercy and forgiveness. When she had finished, she rose.

"God hears all we say. You have told God that you repent, and are sorry. Take care you tell Him no lies, or it will be worse for you. Go now to bed, and sleep. To-night you need have no fear. Come upstairs softly, for fear of waking the house."

She had no fear of the man who a few minutes before would have murdered her, and led the way, clothed in her long white robe, her bare feet glistening upon the stair-carpet, her long hair flowing free; and the man following her unclad and bent, feeble and unsteady, wondering and dazed.

She watched him get into bed, and sat down by the side of it. He tossed and moaned. The foolish nurse in her easy-chair slept steadily and comfortably. Norah laid her hand upon his eyes, whispering, "God has heard our prayer. Think only that you repent, and sleep in peace."

He turned his face upon the pillow—was it in faith, or was it in fatigue?—and slept again.

When the nurse awoke, Norah left him, and went to bed. But in the morning they found their patient in a fever, and raving. Norah told the doctor what had happened.

"My dear young lady, you might have been murdered. The man has got delirium tremens."

So Myles had to put off his holiday, and watched by the bedside of his enemy, who fought and wrestled with the devils that possessed him.

After a week he suddenly got better, and began to talk. Norah, listening to his foolish prattle, heard him go backwards through his life. He began with his evil life on the road, and talked wild nonsense which she did not understand. After a time he began to talk of the army: then of Oxford—when Norah discovered that he was a gentleman by birth: and then of school life. And then he stopped: seemed to recover his senses: picked up his strength, and asked to be allowed to dress and walk about again.

They dressed him and brought him downstairs. He was now the most delightful-looking old man possible to imagine. His hair was long, and of that soft, creamy white which is almost pathetic; his mouth was singularly soft and sweet; his eyes were of a limpid blue; there were no ugly lines about his face: his nose, which had been swollen with drink before his illness, was fine now, and delicate in its shape; his chin was sharp and cleanly shaped; his face was smooth-shaven. Strange to say, too, his manners were perfect, though a little deferent and hesitating. This was explained presently, when they understood that his memory having carried him faithfully back to the period when he was fourteen years of age, stopped there, and left the after part of his life a blank. Mr. Cardiff was only a boy of fourteen. What had happened after that age he forgot; could not possibly recall—made no effort to recall—not any more than a boy at Eton could try to think of a possible past future, *a paulo-post future*, in which he was sixty. They called him Mr. Cardiff, but he made no reply. This astonished them; but after discovering gradually what had befallen him, Miss Ferens thought of asking him his name.

"I am Arthur Vyvyan Dimsdale," he answered with the sweetest possible blush.

"We must call him Arthur," said Norah. "Father, you see that we have a new member of our family."

There was no fear of him; the doctor told them, that such as he was now, he would probably remain till the end came; he showed no vices—he spoke gently and nicely—he drank water by choice—he was delighted to be sent on messages—he would go and buy things for them—he would dig in the garden, and manifested a fine taste for flowers; only he could not bear the sight of a book, and never wanted to read anything. When any one noticed him, he would blush and laugh, like a sensitive boy; he never lost his temper—never was discontented, never sulky. "Altogether," as Miss Ferens said, "the only boy that was ever tolerable."

No one in Esbrough recognised in him the fine delegate from the United States who egged on the workmen to attack young Mr. Armstrong; nor did any of the boys remember him in the gruesome, tottering old man they had chivied through the streets as joyously as the children in Mansoul, since the deliverance of that city, are reported to chivy any unfortunate waif and stray from the camp of Diabolus.

Once Norah was reading from a paper an account of some cruel deed.

The "boy" interrupted her.

"Norah," he said, "don't read any more. How *can* people be so wicked? It is too dreadful to think of."

Evidently a carefully and delicately reared boy.

Then Myles, this event having turned out satisfactorily, grew restless again. He was ashamed of his restlessness; tried to put it down to the score of ill-health, which was absurd, as he had never a day's illness since the well-nigh fatal attack of delirium, and made his own life a burden to himself. Miss Ferens watched him with keen eyes.

"Men are so," she said to Norah. "We are content to go on quietly, the days following one another placidly, with no change. But men are different: they want excitement and change. I have read that men in colonies and quiet country towns go mad sometimes for want of variety in their lives."

"What am I to do?" asked Norah. "I talk

to him; but it never seems to me that I talk with him. He listens, and that is all. My poor father! can we not send him somewhere all by himself?"

"We will let him do what he likes for a month," said Miss Ferens, who had a quiet talk with Myles; the result being that he slipped out of the house, one fine morning in October, his faithful old stick in his hand, and a bag at his back containing his simple toilette materials, and disappeared, leaving the cottage in charge of Miss Ferens and Norah—and the boy, now the most docile, quiet, and genial of all boys.

After a week he came back again, a little weather-beaten about the face, his grizzled locks a little longer, and with an expression of the most profound disappointment.

Norah asked no questions; but after dinner, over his coffee, Myles opened his heart.

"Norah, my princess! you haven't asked me why I came back so soon."

"We waited for you to tell us, father."

"I've nothing to tell, Norah; that is, I've everything to tell, but I don't know how to tell it. I've been to the old places and among the old people, my friends in the days when I was a licensed hawker. They are the same, but I am different. I can't go there any more. It's all you and Jack, I suppose. The life that I have been thinking, for the last six months, so full of pleasure and delight, is gone from me. I can't enjoy it any more. What have you done to me, alaunah?

"I found the cottagers glad to see me, but their ways are coarse and rough. Fancy me, Myles Cuolahan, finding anything coarse and rough. They came to their doors to welcome me; they gave me their best, poor things, but I did not enjoy it. They wanted me to sing and tell them stories, and I was glum and uncomfortable. Then I went into the towns. Norah, my dear, Miss Ferens, you won't need to be told that I couldn't stand the towns. It was all over again. There was another Cardiff Jack—I beg your pardon," he turned to "the boy."

"Why do you beg my pardon, Mr. Cuolahan?" answered the young gentleman with the grey hair. "I do not know any Cardiff Jack."

"No, I suppose you don't," returned Myles,

with a smile. "How should you? Well, there was our old friend, and there was another, General Duckett, and some other rogues and villains, trading on honest people. And to think that once I sat down among them all, thinking no wrong, and never troubled my head about what they did nor how they lived, provided they were good company. There were women among them. God forgive me, Norah. But when I thought of you and Miss Ferens here, and the things I have heard from you both, I could have got up and left the house. It's sick and sad I am to think of what the world is like. And me to be in it so long, and never to know it till now. I've done with roaming. Henceforth I sit at home, if the Lord will." He was silent for a while. Then he got up, and went into Jack's workshop, whither presently Norah followed him. He was sitting with his pipe in his mouth on a wooden stool, in an attitude of profound reflection.

Norah crept behind him, unseen, and laid her hand on his forehead.

"It's only you, darlin' Norah?"

"Only me, father," she replied, pulling

back his head, and kissing him between the eyes.

"I am a pretty sort of man to have a daughter like you."

"Don't, father; you make me unhappy if you talk like that."

"I've got all that a man can ask for. I've got a daughter that's the queen of all women."

"If you say that again I will . . . I will take your pipe out of your mouth."

"It's gone, Norah," he replied, setting it on the lathe. "It's gone. I've got the best of all daughters, and the best of all sons, though he's gone away among the foreigners, and I'm not content. I must needs hanker after the old wild life. Oh! Norah, Norah, if you knew all the shame and degradation of it all. . . . That you can never know."

"You were never shamed and degraded, father."

"Not in any way you can think of, dear. But yet . . . But yet . . . Norah, will you hear your father's confession?"

"No, dear, I would rather not."

"Yes, Norah, for I can't be happy while I

think there is a secret about me you might find out. Listen, dear, and kiss me afterwards if you can. I was once a great drunkard. It was years ago. Jack knows it. He was only nine years old; but he saved your life."

"Jack saved my life?"

"He saved your life, my dear; but it was your father who wanted to take it."

"Oh! father, I cannot believe it."

"It is true, Norah; it is the truth of the blessed Gospels. Don't think that I did not love you always. God knows I did. But I was mad with the drink; and one night I got up more mad than ever, in the middle of the night. I saw you and Jack asleep in the moonlight in each other's arms, and I took the poker to kill you both."

"Poor Jack!" said Norah.

"Then I crept across the room—I remember it all so well, though I was mad—the poker in my hand, and you two, the sweet little children, sound asleep before me. To think of it, Norah, to think of it. . . . Was my heart stone? Was my mind filled with the devil? . . . And I remember I loved you both all the time I was going to do it. And then God waked up Jack. He stood in front of me, my brave boy, his eyes fearless, just as he stood before the raging workmen two months ago. . . . And he said nothing, only he took me by the arm. . . . Why, it might have happened yesterday, so well I remember it all. . . . It was the blessed . . ."

"Not the Blessed Virgin, father."

"No, I forgot I was a Prodesdan then; but whoever it was, it was some one who made me take the pillow for you, and I murdered that entirely with the poker. . . . Oh! Norah, Norah. . . . And the next thing I remember was a long day, which seems a year, and then I was leaning out of the window, when Miss Ferens, God bless her, pulled me back by the coat-tails, and you, that I thought I had murdered, was laughing and crowing in my arms. My darling, my Norah. . . ." He sprang to his feet, and clasped her in his arms. . . . "When I think of it all at night, I cannot do anything, since you taught me the way, but go down upon my knees, and praise God for all His mercies."

"My poor father!" said Norah. "And Miss Ferens knows all?"

"She knows everything, and she said she wouldn't tell; and Jack knows everything, and he pretends he has forgotten. Norah, forgive me."

"There is nothing to forgive, father; but I am thankful to you for telling me."

"It has been on my mind ever since I went away all the last week. I have seen again the wretchedness that the drink does among the people. I had almost forgotten it, Norah. I took the pledge the day after from Father Mathew himself, and I've kept it ever since; but that is not enough. Do you think I, too, could do something for the unhappy men and women, like myself, who destroy and waste their lives with the poison that the public-houses sell them?"

"Think it over, father. Why should you not? But think it over, and . . . and . . . father . . . you have told me all, and I am glad, because I honour you now ten times as much as ever I did before. But don't talk of it any more. Don't let me hear about it again. It is a past horror. It is a great sin, repented of, and forgiven."

"You think that God forgives such sins?"

"Is there any sin that God will not forgive? Father, we are Christians."

"Yes, but you have never sinned."

"Oh! father, don't say that. You do not know the heart of a girl, or you would not say it. Leave off thinking me your queen, as you call it. Think of me only as your daughter, full of faults, and only trying to do her best, and . . . and . . . go on loving me. It is love that I want."

"And love that you have, my angel from Paradise. We all love you. I love you with all my heart, for I think of you every hour of the day; I dream of you every hour of the night; all my life is yours, Norah. When I pray to God, it is for my daughter, who is taking me to heaven with her."

"Father, father, I don't deserve it."

"When I thank God, it is for you; and Jack loves you too."

"Ah! yes," murmured the girl, her eyes filling with tears, "Jack loves me too."

CHAPTER XIV.

Miss Ferens stayed on in Esbrough. For the first time she was in a life of reality. This was what the books talked of, the crowd of workers, the hive of bees, that seemed from a distance to hum so harmoniously, and yet were so full each of his own personal hopes, envies, jealousies, and fears. It is by the blending of all these notes—there are not a great many in the gamut of human passion—that the harmonious effect is produced. It amused the lady, come into the busy manufacturing town from her quiet cathedral city, to watch what she could of all its humours; she admired the arrogant kingliness of Paul Bayliss, the quiet assumption of his rank by Captain Perrymont; she saw how

> "All conditions and all minds
> (As well of glib and slippery creatures as
> Of grave and austere quality) tender down
> Their services to—— "

these two mighty princes. And then she turned her eyes homewards, and saw with amazement, as well as with interest, the little comedy that was being played before her own eyes, in which Norah took the principal part, and, in the absence of Jack, Frank Perrymont was the hero. The plot of the play was that Norah had set herself to persuade Frank to be in love with Ella Bayliss; and if this were done, another difficulty remained behind, to persuade Ella to accept Frank.

The Captain did not think proper to tell his son the result of his "experiments" with Norah, and on being questioned, gravely replied that Frank had better make his own experiments for himself, which the young man proceeded to do in the manner usual among suitors. For he called at the cottage; he made a particular friend of Miles Cuolahan ; he waylaid Miss Ferens and bestowed bouquets upon that lady, to her intense amazement; he wrote verses with the most ardent breath of passion, and offered them at the shrine of the adored one. Norah, inexperienced, save by the teachings of that instinct which never fails a woman, in the arts of flirtation and modern courtship, at first paid little heed to what she thought would be a passing fancy. But it was no passing fancy, and Frank Perrymont, for the first time in his life, was serious. Ella Bayliss saw it with the mixed delight which comes of having what you want and yet not getting it your own way. Most things in this world are so, chiefly because so many unreasonable people want exactly the same thing as ourselves. You see it was not altogether pleasant to think of an old admirer going over to another woman, even although the desertion seems to leave the coast clear for other and more desirable arrangements. Fortunately, Ella did not know, nor did any one know, the whole extent of the desertion. Only Norah knew, and she was silent about it.

"Why do you bring me these verses?" she asked one day, receiving a sheet of rhymes addressed to "Aura," which the fond swain adopted because it could so easily be changed, on occasion, into Norah. "I am the worst of critics, Mr. Perrymont, even if you are the best of poets. Do you want me to tell you the faults and the beauties of the verses? They seem to me rather weak, you know, though they are certainly pretty. Have I not seen most of the lines before, or some of them? All the new poets seem to me to make up their poems bit by bit, cento fashion, out of the old ones. Perhaps the old ones did the same out of the older ones."

"I do not want you to criticise," said Frank, rather hurt at this plain speaking. "Can you not see that I try to throw my soul into my verse?"

"Yes, I see that," said Norah, pitilessly. "Do not you think it rather selfish of young verse-writers to expect sympathy from the world because they *try* to throw their soul into their rhymes?"

"I do not expect sympathy from the world. I—I—hoped that I might get it from you."

She hardened her soul. He had her sympathy, because he looked so longing and so unhappy, but she would not tell him so.

"But suppose, Mr. Perrymont, that I do not want to read your soul? I have many things to think of and to do. On the whole, I have not time to read into the souls of more than a few people. I like to know what my dear Susan is thinking of, and what my father feels about things—and—but that is nearly all."

"Is there no way," asked Frank, "to touch your heart?"

"My heart," repeated Norah, with a quick flush. "It is touched by everything, I think. Do you mean that I am cold and selfish?"

"Not selfish: only cold—cold to me."

Norah hesitated a moment. Then she replied, without shame or blushing—

"Not cold, Frank Perrymont, because I take a great interest in you; but—I do not know whether you are only practising a little flirtation with me——"

"No—a thousand times no!"

"I believe you are not, because I know you are a gentleman, and because, though I do not think your verses very good, they seem to me to show something of your character. Then, Frank Perrymont, I will answer you before you have questioned me. You want to make love to me. Do not."

"Why not, Norah? Let me call you Norah, for once."

"You may call me Norah all your life, if it will give you any pleasure. But do not ask me to love you, because—because I cannot."

"You cannot. Oh, Norah! you think you cannot. It is the caprice of a girl. Woman's love rises to meet love: woman's passion sleeps till her lover wakens it. Let me only love you, and trust that you will soon love me."

She shook her head.

"No, Frank. It is impossible. You mistake altogether. My poor boy, you would be miserable with me. You are led astray by some blindness. It is not me you love at all. It is another girl. You have written so much verse that your Aura, whom you describe there with black eyes and all the rest of it, seems to your brain to resemble me. Leave the world of fancy and come back to the world of fact. Tell me, were you not in love with some one else before you saw me?"

Frank said nothing.

"I am sure of it. I saw it the first time I met you. And I know who it is. Frank Perrymont, it is—shall I tell you?"

"What does it matter?" he answered stupidly.

"It is Ella Bayliss. Long before you knew me, Ella's face was in your thoughts, Ella's eyes before your own. I am certain of it. Tell me truly, was it not so?"

"I once thought I loved her."

"Then you love her still, and what you were going to say to me was the wilful treachery of love. Frank Perrymont, you ought to be ashamed of yourself."

"But I do not love her still," he answered passionately. "She is not like you. Norah, I love you. I live in the divine tenderness of your voice. I see all the depths of love in your eyes—I feel——"

"You feel all the unreal rapture of a poet who sets up an ideal, my poor boy," she said, with the superiority of nineteen over four and twenty. "You wanted a peg: Ella Bayliss—*the girl you love*—must be wooed and won in proper fashion, and as girls ought to be, through the permission of her father, and then you would see, what is it?—I quote your own words—her love rising to meet your love: her sleeping passion wakened by your words.

Frank Perrymont, what have I done or said that you should make me your Lesbia, your Chloe, your Dulcinea? I think, sir, you have insulted me."

"No, Norah! no."

"Then you have made a great mistake about me. You have fancied that I was a girl to step between you and your bride-presumptive. Why did you think so?"

"Good heavens! You talk as if I were in love with Ella."

"You have just told me you thought you were in love with her.. Men who fancy they are in love with girls and make them fancy so, and then go off to somebody else, do not seem to me worth having. Mr. Frank Perrymont, if I were to listen to you—which is impossible, quite impossible, and always was—in a week you might be in love with Ella again. I do not like will-o'-the-wisps."

Frank was silent and confused. The girl's sharp wit caught him at all points.

"I was wrong," he said at last. "Give me my verses, Norah."

"No, I shall keep your verses, because they are pretty, and I do not often get pretty verses written all for my own special criticism. But you shall have a copy, if you will, to give to Ella."

He held his peace.

"To give to Ella, Mr. Perrymont. You hear me?"

"Yes—no, I mean, Miss Cuolahan. Undoubtedly I hear you."

"I am glad we have dropped the Christian names, because I do not think we are going to be friends at all. I am a girl inexperienced in the world, Mr. Perrymont, as you know, and only belonging to society on a sort of sufferance, which our friends in this town would very soon put an end to, if they could; but I like a man to be honourable in his court to a woman."

"You say that I am dishonourable?"

"Do not let us quarrel," she returned, with a grave smile. "You see, if I were a man, we could fight. No, fighting is gone out of fashion. Gentlemen, nowadays, I believe, swear largely and bang out of the room. You will hardly do that with me. I am going to speak my whole mind. Now listen, my young poet, and I will tell you something about women, which you may put into verse, and it will be a great deal more poetical than unreal raptures about impossible passion. Women very seldom fall in love of their own accord with any one. We are brought up as if passion was not in existence. Fathers and mothers, governesses and guardians, aunts and goody-goody books all go on as if girls had no hearts; as if love was a thing which does not exist. So that all we know is from novels, and that is not much, novelists being such extremely foolish creatures, as a rule. Charles Reade can draw a woman, but he is the only man among them all who knows what a woman is like—unless it be Anthony Trollope, and his girls are only pasteboard conventionalities. Presently, you see, there comes down from the army or the university, just as you came down here, a young gentleman who begins to make love. Pray, on whom did you try your 'prentice hand, Mr. Frank Perrymont?"

Frank laughed.

"Go on, Miss Cuolahan. Ella wasn't the first."

"Then you ought to be more ashamed of

yourself than you are, and"—she burst out laughing—" if I were your sister, I would box your depraved ears, sir. Now be quiet, till I tell you."

She had the least little bit of an Irish phrase, here and there, which she had picked up from her father.

"He comes down, Monsieur Chevalier, and begins to make love. Then the girl gets uneasy. Nothing in her education has prepared her for this curious feeling. She is attracted, and she is frightened. She is afraid of making advances, and she is afraid of seeming cold. If he leaves her there, if he entices her heart out of the calm fold of passionless make-believe in which they have educated her, he dooms her to certain misery. Frank Perrymont, there is a greater unhappiness than the memory of lost joys—it is the thought of joys that might have been."

She spoke half in jest and half in earnest, but her eyes filled with tears.

"Norah," said Frank, after a pause, "you speak from knowledge. You, too——"

"Hush!" she cried. "Some day, people will change it all. They will bring boys and girls up together, as they do in America, so that they shall not be so ignorant of each other's natures, and so ashamed to look into each other's souls. They will teach the children that the rose and crown of life is love—that, like all the prizes of this world, it is greatly to be desired and to be prayed for; that it does not come for all; but that all must work and make themselves ready for it, looking on their life as due, not to themselves, but to their lovers. Ah! Frank, help the happy time and be true to yourself."

"Tell me, Norah——"

"No, I will tell you nothing. Yes, Frank, I will tell you something, because you are a gentleman and will ask no questions, and tell no one, and try not to guess at anything. I have said all this out of my own heart. It is because I love . . . I love . . . a man . . ." She did not blush, but the words dropped from her lips with a soft lingering, while her eyes were suffused with a softness which spoke of tears in the background. "I love a man whose name you may not ask. He loves me too, but we shall, perhaps, never marry. I think, you see, of what might be, and—and,

Frank, I am not happy. Do not try to move me any more. Perhaps you were mistaken. Perhaps—let me be honest with you —I want you to marry Ella Bayliss. After all, what can you do better for yourself? If she loves you, there is beauty, and there is wealth."

The young man made a gesture of impatience.

"Let us finish, Miss Cuolahan. If I cannot have you, do not advise me—I shall go my own way."

"Do not be angry, Frank."

He passed from one extreme to another, and seizing her little hand, kissed it passionately.

"I will do all you like, everything you like, Norah, and for your sake. Bid me marry Ella Bayliss, if you will, and I will marry her. I would even marry that woman opposite, Mrs. Merrion, if you told me."

Norah turned pale.

"No, Frank, I don't think I should like you to marry her, of all women. Now go. Forget all that we have said, and think of me only as a friend. I suppose men and women may possibly be friends—may they not?—without always wanting to be in love. It is a fault of our defective education if they cannot, because we are not taught definitively that each can only belong to one. Yes, Frank, for more reasons than one, I want you to marry the girl with whom you were once in love. I want it for. her sake, to prevent her falling into misery and disappointment. And I want it—for my own."

Frank went away—feeling something like the young man who was ordered to sell all he had and give to the poor. For Ella Bayliss was not now his ideal, and Norah was. Only his imagination, easily excited, as easily shifted its ground. Perhaps, if women were wise, they would be shy of marrying poets and young gentlemen of poetic proclivities; for their inclinations are like the point of the weathercock. Frank went to call at the Hall. Ella was alone, daintily dressed, and disposed to *bouder* with her old admirer. But then Jack had been away for three months, and one must keep one's hand in. When he went away he had already deflected many points, and if Norah should be west, and Ella south, his position might be expressed as sou'-west by south.

"Have I said too much?" asked Norah. "Will he think that I have been rude and unmaidenly?"

And made herself unhappy all the morning, thinking over possible sins.

Then came a letter from Jack, all to herself, and the first she had ever received from him.

"My dearest Norah,

"I hear from Myles—from your father, I mean, only I always call him Myles, and cannot help it—who gives me all the news he can think of: I hear from Mr. Bayliss, who is anxious to know how I am getting on in my quest: I hear even from Mr. Hodder, our foreman, who stood by us on that day when you behaved like Deborah and became a prophetess. I hear from—from some one who I wish had forgotten me. But I never hear from you. Write to me sometimes, if only to let me know that you have not quite forgotten me. It would be better for you if you had, because I have thrown away my chances, and have no right even to a kind thought from you. Norah, I wish at times that I had not spoken to you as I did—and then I am glad that I did. It was wrong to tell you that I love you, with such a frightful obstacle in the way, one that I do not see my way out of; but then it was a happiness greater than I can hope to make you understand, only to tell you. All the world is different to me since then—I work better, I think better, I see better. Between you and me there rises the spectre of a promise, given in a foolish moment, and yet that must be kept. You know, dear Norah, that I have bound myself. It was Mr. Fortescue's only lesson —always to keep my word. He began it the first day I went to him, and has never ceased repeating it. 'Keep your word,' he used to say; 'it is the secret of all happiness. To keep your word means honour, duty, obedience, and everything. Keep your word.' Let what will happen, I must keep my word, till I am released. But I cannot bind you. You are free, Norah. No syllable of sorrow shall escape from my lips, or from my eyes, even when you find another man whom you can love better than myself. And you will help me to bear my burden, the only one that I have. Norah, I believe I am going to make myself rich. I have found, among the ironworks of these Prussians, the secret that I looked for. It is not an actual secret, because every one well knows the method. But I think that I alone know how to carry it out. Is it because I was born in the old furnace-room that I seem to have an instinct about iron? I think it must be. This is my secret. I can turn the commonest English iron into the best. I can make of the worst metal we put into a furnace the best that was ever forged into a Krupp. I stand over the furnace and put in the manganese, that does it. I know how much to put in, and I know when to do it. I will tell all the world how much is wanted, but no one except myself knows the right moment to put it in. How do I know it? I seem to feel it. I know the colour, the heat, the fumes, and if I fail at the exact moment of time, the metal is hopelessly ruined. How the power came to me I do not know, but it is as certain as that I can read and write. And I am coming home to make the best use of my power. For I mean to be rich.

"Do you think I am mercenary? I do not. It seems to me that to make himself rich is the duty of a man in these times. I know that wealth means self-indulgence with most people, but I try to think it will not with me. I think of all that wealth can do; how it can relieve the thriftless, and help the thrifty, and aid civilization; and I want wealth to make experiments with. I belong to the very lowest stratum, because I was brought up among the people who suffer most, and I feel for them and with them. The memory of the early days never leaves me: I remember the days of tramp along the roads, when every other word was a word of complaint; I remember the men who drank and the women who lamented; I remember the suffering and the sorrow. And then I know the lives of the hands. They might be so entirely beautiful—their lives, were it not for the vices of the men, their prodigality, their selfishness, and their drink. Norah, whatever we may be to each other henceforth, let us be friends in this: I promise you that if I make money, I will help, so far as I can, the men and women about me.

"Norah, a thought often comes over me. What if we were all of us to resolve always to give to everybody in want, and always to forgive every one who trespassed against us. Would not people cease to sin and to be idle for very shame? I cannot think that there is any man who deliberately makes evil his good. I should like to take some poor wretch from the road—I remember the kind of man exactly; ferocious, wild-eyed, haggard with drink and want—and, after dressing him daintily, place him in a kind of prison where he would have to associate with people of gentle life. Do you not think that after a time he would be humanised, and would look back upon the shameful past with a sort of horror? Or there are women—those terrible women that one sees in great cities and reads of in books, say, of the French Revolution. How would it be to take one of them, and make her clean and dress her becomingly, and seat her with ladies for six months, till perforce her language was purified and her heart cleansed? What else is meant when Christ bade us turn the other cheek, and give the other half of the stolen garment? And yet it is nearly two thousand years ago and we have never even tried it. Religion has yet to reign, some time, in the world, and perhaps the doctrine of social pardon may come in at last.

"How is it, Norah, that I can say to you what I can say to no one else? The thoughts that come into my head are kept all to myself, except to you. I dare not tell you some because I have no right, but those that I do tell you are what I can tell to no other living creature. If I weary you with my egotism, let me know, and I will write no more.

"And now, Norah, my—sister. Since it must be so, let us be brother and sister again, and tell each other everything. The veil that was between us is lowered: the cloud that had grown up during the year of separation is dissipated. You know me now, as you did when you were a child: you trust me, as you did then: I know you too, Norah, now. Write to me. Just once. I shall be home again sooner than you think, but not before you have time to write me.

"JACK."

The girl read the letter. Alone in the garden, where the barren branches of the apple-trees grated against each other under the cold autumn wind; her face flushed and heated, her heart beating, her pulses bounding, her blood coursing through her veins. It was her first love-letter: a strange love-letter, but yet breathing love in every word.

"He loves me," she murmured, gazing round her with eyes that saw nothing, but limpid and clear—those black eyes, wells of light and softness to those whom they love, stony-hearted Arctic Oceans to those whom they love not. "He loves me, he loves me always."

And then by a natural revulsion, her thoughts turned to where "the other woman" was sitting, also waiting the return of her betrothed.

"No," she whispered savagely. "She shall not have him. She shall not have him. I will kill her first. I would rather see my Jack dead in his grave. I would rather—oh! God forgive me. God forgive me for a selfish girl." And then she thought of Mrs. Bastable and what she had said, and took comfort.

She spent the whole afternoon in writing a reply. It was very short, but it was all she could say.

"Dear Jack," it went. "Come home as soon as you can, sooner than you can if that is possible. We all want you—Myles, and Miss Ferens, and your "—sister she was going to write, but crossed it out, with a shudder. "Your affectionate Norah."

CHAPTER XV.

It was on a cold and rainy afternoon in December that Jack came home again. Norah was sitting at the window, her work in her lap, looking sadly out on the dreary prospect. There was no colour in anything: the flowers were dead: the grey and leaden clouds hung over the sky, weighed down by the smoke of the factories: her own life loomed before her like some long voyage over sunless seas beaten into sullen waves by a gale that had no end: what was the use of it all—what was the meaning of it all? The girl was weighed down by the solemn problem that comes to every one of us when life is at its darkest. What was the meaning of it all? At such moments the highest aspirations seem foolish, the dreams of the past are vain, the very things we most delight in lose their joy and the things we most fear are loaded with ten times their normal weight of horror. Then comes the sunshine of heaven, and straight the spring time is on our hearts, the rain is over and done, the frosts are broken up, and all the world sings one great and glorious pæan of praise to God. For things are what we fancy them, and what the gloomy thoughts of an unquiet spirit clothes with cloud, the brightness of hope decks with all the colours of a tropical sunrise. Have you ever driven at early morning along a valley which the night has filled with fog and watched the sun chase away the mists? Wave upon wave they rise and seem to roll along the depths swiftly and more swiftly, till what was inpenetrable cloud bursts by magic into river edged with green and glancing wood, more beautiful than any poet's dream.

Jack returned. Norah saw him with his strong elastic tread, and her heart flew up. In a moment he was with her and she was in his arms.

"Norah," he whispered, "it is nonsense. We are not brother and sister. We are lovers. I love you: I love you."

She answered nothing. Only her cheek lay against his: his hand was on her hair smoothing it back: his lips were touching hers: his strong arm was round her. He kissed her again and again, while the red blood flew to her face and back again to her heart; while her pulses beat quicker; while she glowed from head to foot with the happiness that comes but once in a life, and only then when the heart is fresh and pure.

"I have tried to make it otherwise, my darling," said her lover. "I have thought of —of what lies between us. But I can do nothing else than love you. Tell me, dear —tell me."

"Yes, Jack," she answered. "Yes, I love you too; as much as you can love me, and more. I think of you as much as you can think of me, and more. I long to see you and to have you with me, as much as you can for me, and more. But, Jack, Jack, it is wrong; it is impossible."

He let her go for a moment, and looked across the room with a groan. He might have seen, had he suspected, the corner of a blind displaced, and behind it an opera glass, through which his *fiancée* was curiously gazing upon the scene. But it was as well for him that he did not, and better still that he did not see the face behind the glass, white with rage and disappointment.

"It shall not be impossible, Norah," Jack ground out between his teeth. "I will put an end to it;. I will release myself from bondage."

But Norah had had time to freeze again, as becomes a young lady.

"No, Jack; talk of something else. I was wrong; only, perhaps I could not help it. Let us remember our happiness; we have kissed each other, have we not? And what else has life to offer? Tell me of yourself. No, Jack; I will not, indeed. Sit down—so, a good two yards away. And now tell me about yourself. What have you brought from Germany?"

"I have brought my new power with me that I told you of, Norah. Yes, I shall be rich, because I know how to make other people rich. I shall sell my knowledge to the highest bidder; and when I am rich—when I have sold it——"

"Then, Jack, we will face the question of the—woman over the way."

Norah was as gentle as any girl in the United Kingdom, except on one subject. Mrs. Merrion was "the woman."

"And till then—till then we have to face it boldly. Let us say no more about it."

"Only this, Norah; I have begged her to release me, and she refuses."

"Perhaps," said Norah, "she will not refuse when others have to beg. No, sir; I will not explain what I mean. Tell me more about your life in Germany. How do you like the Germans, and are the German ladies pretty?"

In the evening a note came for Jack, which, fortunately for Norah's peace of mind, she did not see. It was not extraordinary that he should have to go into the town, and she saw him go, without a suspicion that he was about to cross the road and go straight to "the woman's" house. Which, however, Jack did, while Norah and her white-headed boy sat down to a game of dominoes, and Myles retreated to the workshop for his evening pipe.

"I like Jack," said Mr. Cardiff, arranging his dominoes. "I like Jack very much. When I grow up I shall be an engineer. I used to think that I would be a soldier, but I've changed my mind. Double sixes. Now I'm going to beat you again, Norah dear. Six-five. You see, after all a soldier's life has nothing noble about it, except when you fight for your country."

"Every life is noble if we choose to make it so," said his instructress, who lost no opportunity of impressing a moral upon her pupil.

"I dare say; but some lives are more noble than others. I should like a life where you are always doing good in some way or other; making other people happier, and reforming wicked people. Do you think any wicked people are ever really happy, Norah?"

"I should think not. No one can be happy unless he is trying to make himself better every day."

"That is what I say to myself night and morning," replied the boy, with a beautiful look of faith and hope upon his face. "That is what I say to myself. Oh! why cannot

everybody agree to help each other, Norah?
I was reading yesterday about the criminal
classes. The writer said that there were I
don't know how many thousands who live by
preying on honest people. Think of that.
Preying on honest people; it sounds so
dreadful."

And so on; the talk which went on every
day while the gentle old man, with his mind
fixed at the age of thirteen or so, poured out
the long thoughts that fill the brain of a
clever and imaginative boy. He had read,
this boy; could quote the poetry of Felicia
Hemans, weeping over the sorrowful tale of
Casabianca; would even, in the garden, play
by himself at being Robinson Crusoe, building
a hut. He had good manners, and knew a
gentleman when he saw one. That was the
reason why, secretly, he did not like Norah's
papa, Myles Cuolahan, in whom he saw little
points of behaviour of which he could not
approve. It was also the reason why he
was greatly taken with Jack—the ideal of
a boy, tall, handsome, and clever, and able to
make things. He was a great comfort to
Norah in these times, and she had fallen so

completely into the old man's delusion that he was still a boy, that she regarded him as one, and was quite content to believe boyhood consistent with white hair and a feeble step. For Mr. Cardiff was growing very feeble. At nine, or even earlier, he went to bed, after a glass of milk, which he accepted with as much joy and gratitude as if strong waters did not exist and the grape had never been invented.

So Jack left the two to their devices, and went across the road. Mrs. Merrion had by this time recovered her temper.

"You see, Jenny," said Keziah, on learning from her cousin that Jack had returned and had actually been kissing Norah—"at the very window! before my own eyes!"—"you see, Jenny, the boy's nothing to you, nor never will be."

"Keziah, you're a fool!" returned Jenny, "and always were a fool. Who but a fool would have married a Benjamin Bastable?"

"I was a fool then," said Keziah. "But— but I should be a Solomon in petticoats and a false front, compared with Jack Armstrong, if he were to think of marrying you, Jenny.

Why, you're double his age, pretty near. Don't use bad language, because it isn't becoming. You know you're thirty-five, if you are a day, and he's twenty-two, or it may be twenty-four."

"He's twenty-six," said Jenny, "and I'm thirty. And you had better not drive me into a rage,.Keziah: I'm a meek woman enough when you let me alone."

"I know your meekness, Jenny," returned the other. "Mighty meek you are at all times: and I'm the only one that isn't afraid of you when you are not meek. Lord bless you, Jenny! what's the use of tantrums with me? Why shouldn't Jack kiss Norah? They're almost brother and sister: and if they were husband and wife, they'd make the prettiest couple that ever was seen. Come, don't be a fool, Jenny. Try the old ones as much as you like."

Jenny flung herself out of the room with a slam, upsetting two chairs in her transit. These Keziah picked up, and went on with her work quietly.

When Jack came at her bidding, she was dressed in her best and quietest. The room was lit with a soft moderator lamp; a bright fire burned; there was the odour of fragrant coffee; and Adelaide, in black velvet, sat in her low chair by the fireside, a volume of poetry in her hand, looking a little flushed by the heat of the fire perhaps, or else from the emotion caused by the return of her betrothed. Her face, seen by artificial light, had a sort of velvety smoothness about it; and her eyes, dark, deep, and lustrous, promised mines of love and constancy. She turned them full upon Jack—an artillery which once he could not resist.

"You are back, then?" she murmured, giving him her hand, which he could not choose but take. "You are back, and you did not come to see me till I had sent for you."

"I did not," said Jack.

"And you have no word of kindness for me?" she whispered, holding his hand in hers, and bending her face so that the light should catch her profile and glance upon her lustrous hair—a *tour de force* in coquetry which this inimitable woman had acquired after many years of practice with a hand-mirror. "No single word for your Adelaide? —your betrothed?"

He was silent.

"Tell me, Jack," she murmured, in her softest voice. "Tell me that you did not mean that cruel letter you wrote to me. It was so hard!—so bitter to bear! I read it with all the others I have from you. You have forgotten them, perhaps; but I keep them all. A lover's letters are so sacred that I keep every one. I never had any but yours, because the General married me without giving himself time to write love-letters."

That, at least, was true. In her desk were no letters from any General Merrion.

"I have got them all," she went on, kissing his hand and holding it still. "There is one in which you say that nothing shall ever part us—not sorrow, nor sickness, nor any other woman. Ah! it makes me happy to read it! Shall I show this letter to your—*sister*, Jack?"

"I have no sister," he replied.

"I mean Norah; your sister by adoption. She is a sweet girl, and is going to marry Frank Perrymont, I believe."

"Come, Adelaide," said Jack, snatching his hand from the soft and padded fetters of her fingers: "come, Adelaide, let us have an explanation."

"No; I will have no explanation."

"Can you not see that it is impossible?"

"No, I cannot; and I will not. You are, I admit, a little younger than myself. You are twenty-three, and I am nearly twenty-seven. I wish the difference was the other way; but we cannot help that. There is no impossibility, Jack, my dearest, when two people love each other."

"But when they do not?"

"That I am not concerned with. You love me: you have given me a thousand proofs—in letters. And I love you: I have given you as many proofs of that—in letters."

Jack groaned. Then he sat down, his head in his hands, and looked at her.

"You refuse to release me, do you?"

"I refuse to release you, Mr. Armstrong," she replied, in a hard voice, different to the soft tones in which she had been speaking. "I utterly refuse to release you."

"Then," said Jack, rising, "I shall take the course that seems best to me."

"And I," she replied, rising too, and facing him, "shall take the course that seems best to me. We have been engaged for five years. You have written to me, during all that time, letters of the most ardent affection. I have wasted my time upon you, refused to receive others whose intentions were honourable, and compromised, perhaps, the reputation of a life."

Jack looked up and smiled.

She saw him smile, and would have changed colour, but for the fixity of the protecting paint.

"That is all nothing," she went on, "provided you keep your engagement as an honourable man should. Go now, Jack Armstrong, go home and think it over. Will you be a liar and a cheat, or will you be a man of honour? Will you keep the promises of five years, or will you give way to a passing passion for—for that—that"—here her temper grew the better of her—"that black-haired daughter of an Irish pedlar?"

"We will not," said Jack, "introduce any names into our discussion. I will go. And, Adelaide, it is the last time that I enter this house. My mind is made up. I have appealed to you in vain. I cannot love you. I cannot marry you. It is impossible for me to keep my word. And you must do what you think best."

"I have read," replied his Adelaide, "of women who worked spells to bring their lovers back. I have need of none. See, Jack, you will come back to me of your own accord. Look," and she threw herself at his feet, "here are the hands you have kissed so often, and the white arms you have praised. Do you forget that you have knelt at my feet and kissed them? Are my eyes grown dull? Is my cheek wrinkled? Are my lips thin and shrivelled? Is my figure shrunk and wasted? Is my hair false or grey? Have my teeth dropped out? Where is it, Jack, the love that once made you clasp me in your arms a thousand times, and kiss me till the love flew into my heart? Where is it, oh, my Jack, my handsome boy, the only man of all that ever I loved and longed to win? You will kiss me again, Jack, will you not? You will throw your arms round me, my darling?"

Her passion was not simulated. Unreal in everything else, her life a living lie, her history a tissue of deceits, the woman had found, when she should have been a staid matron, a master-passion that held her enthralled and bound her with a rod of iron. She sprang from her knees and threw herself upon Jack's breast, clutching him round the neck with her two white arms. He stood unmoved. The woman's influence was wholly gone. Time was that at the touch of her hand he would thrill: at the rustle of her dress his pulses would move more quickly; but now it was all changed, and he saw her what she was, the woman past her prime, a made-up imitation of a lady, coarse and common, vulgar and unrestrained. She took his hand and laid it against her cheek. He disengaged her gently but firmly, and pointed to his fingers, where she had laid them on her cheek.

"See," he said, "your cheek is painted. You wash off your pretended love just as you wash off your rouge. Let me go."

"Is it peace or war?"

"I am the stronger," said Jack, "because you can do me no real harm. Let it be peace, if you let me go. It shall be war if you refuse. You may think what you have to gain, and what you have to lose. I will even, if you like, tell the world that you have refused me——'"

She made a gesture of impatience.

"The world—the world—what have I ever cared for the world? I want your love. Give me that and I will give you back your letters," she whispered in his ear. But he drew back and answered nothing.

"Then war—war—war!" she cried. "And all the town shall ring with the passion of Jack Armstrong's letters. Two hundred of them, Jack; two hundred! And before the Court they shall all be read, every one!"

Jack said nothing, but was gone while yet she stood, with the words hissing from her mouth, a queen of passion, sublime in her unbounded wrath. Then she heard the door shut as he left the house, and sitting down before the fire, revolved plans of vengeance.

CHAPTER XVI.

JACK went home, with a mind strangely disquieted. It was all true, and exactly as Mrs. Merrion said. He had written letters by the score, all of them love letters, and mostly letters of passionate love. Jack was one who, living in the present, worked hard and enjoyed hard. It had been sweet for him just to be in the presence of the Siren : there had been a time when his brain reeled at the touch of her hand. Now—now—what had caused the change ? It was not that he loved her less, but that he absolutely loathed her : she, though she could not yet realize the fact, had lost her power over him ; there was not even a feeling of pity left. He was disgusted that he had been the prey of a woman so common and so unreal : he was ashamed that he had poured out his thoughts and feelings so freely and frankly. As he paced up and down the little room, he thought of the fair girl lying near him, with but a wall between them, and he groaned when he thought of the things he had said to Mrs. Merrion which should have been kept for Norah. Had he but known! Did we know the possible consequences of any single act, we should never act at all. It is the blessed prerogative of human nature not to know the future. And since there seems no act that we can commit which does not do mischief to some one, there is every reason to believe that the world would fall into a lethargy, and so our race gradually become extinguished, could we calculate the consequences. Those that Jack had to face were a bundle of letters, with all that an angry woman could do. Jack was liable to be paraded in a court of law, his letters of passion read aloud, and his devotion laughed at. Most men would prefer a quiet five minutes or so under the nine-tailed cat, so that no one knew about it, to such ridicule. Jack certainly would have taken punishment with far more alacrity than the ridicule. He passed a bad night pondering over what he could do, and finally fell asleep after, for the hundredth time, assuring himself that nothing, not even public exposure, should make him keep his promise.

Norah met him at breakfast in the morning, her eyes ringed with black, her cheeks pale. She too, had been lying awake, thinking, scheming, and regretting, listening to the tramp of Jack up and down his room, and knowing that there was another creature in the world as anxious as herself. That was, somehow, a comfort, because they were both anxious about the same thing. If one has a toothache, one bears it better if somebody else in the house has one too. They compare the pangs, and together curse their fate.

They greeted each other with downcast eyes, as if they had sinned and were ashamed. Fancy Adam and Eve waking up the morning after that fatal business of theirs—perhaps a little unwell in consequence of the change in diet, and certainly apprehensive of other consequences. Norah and Jack had plucked together the apple of love, and it was from a forbidden tree, because Jack had already gathered the fruit with another. Whatever

Adam's shortcomings, in this, at least, he was better than Jack, that he had but one to share his guilt. Lilith came afterwards, if you remember.

Mr. Cardiff—or rather Arthur Vyvyan Dimsdale—was up before them, and, with mind intent on the importance of the task, was fashioning a model yacht which he proposed to sail in ponds some time during the spring.

"You shall show me how to sail her, Jack," he said with the confidence of a boy in a senior's powers. "I think she shall be cutter-rigged. The last one I had I sailed at the back of the Grange in . . . no——" he stopped and looked round. The only sign of his mental decay was that he sometimes confused places, and was pulled up short by finding himself not in the house where he was born, but quite a different place.

"Never mind the yacht now, Arthur," said Norah. "Let us have breakfast. Have you seen my father?"

"Myles had his breakfast an hour ago," said the boy, placing his toy on a chair, "and I'm jolly hungry."

In spite of his amazing twist, the old man

did not venture to do a very great stroke of breakfast, but presently rose with a robust air and determined face, as one who was bent on enjoying the whole freedom of his holiday in running and jumping. Jack noticed how his legs trembled as he ran from the room.

"Don't take any notice, Jack," said Norah. "It is better so. He is getting feebler every day."

Presently he came back, and sat down wearily.

"Norah," he said, after a pause, "I wonder if I am going to die. I remember reading a story about a boy who died at thirteen. He used to get tired, and then sit down and fall asleep. And after a little he was too weak to get out of bed. And then he died."

"You would not be afraid to die, Arthur, would you?"

He thought for a moment.

"No, Norah; not afraid; not that; only I would rather live."

She spent the morning in conversation over things high and solemn, while his eyes glowed with the light of faith and hope.

"If I live, Norah dear," he said at last, taking her hand—"if I live, I will be a great preacher, and bring the world from wickedness. If I die . . . " he paused.

"If you die, Arthur."

"If I die, I shall go to heaven, shall I not, Norah?—and then we shall all meet, you and I, and—and cousin Lucy—and—where is my cousin Lucy?" He looked round with a dazed air, and then closing his eyes, lay back gently on the sofa and fell fast asleep. As he lay there with a face out of which every crow's-foot had been smoothed out, the long white hair falling back from his forehead, the lips half parted in a smile, there was a boyish look about him which was most curious. Norah sat watching him. She had grown fond of this poor waif and stray of fallen humanity. He had been stricken at her very feet: reduced to a condition in which he could do no harm, driven, perforce, back to a state of innocency, passed through the waters of Lethe, and made ignorant once more of evil. If for every sin into which manhood falls there is some animal which may be taken as its type and personification, then had Cardiff Jack been pig, wolf, tiger, and crocodile, each and all in turn, and now he was once more the bleating lamb.

Jack left them and went to see his old employer at the works. The men nodded to him in their independent and half-respectful way. Mr. Hodder came from his den and timidly shook hands with him; the furnaces, his old friends, seemed to fan themselves into a fierce heat, and the engines to puff and snort a welcome. The young man forgot his gloomy thoughts, and pulled himself together.

"Bah!" he said. "Let her do what she likes. Let her publish all the letters. I will laugh with the rest. Here is work, which is better than love."

All night he had been awake thinking of Norah and the other: now, he shook off the troubles of his loves as he would have taken off his coat. Norah, at home, was sitting in sadness, wretched because Jack was wretched; picturing him lonely in his grief and distracted from his usual work. Mrs. Merrion, selecting and reading his letters, was rejoicing over the misery she was going to bring upon him. And here he was with light heart and unclouded brow, stepping into the works of Bayliss's iron foundry, with his brain running undisturbed and in the usual channels. Mr. Bayliss was in his office. He looked up from the work he was engaged in, and gave Jack a friendly nod.

"Glad to see you back, Armstrong. Wait a moment. . . . Now, then, my lad, for an account of yourself."

"I've been to Germany, and I've come back."

"With empty hands?"

"No, with full hands. I can do it, Mr. Bayliss."

Mr. Bayliss, instinctively, rose and shut the door.

"Now," he said, "let us have it out. I remember! I remember. You were going to make English steel as good as Prussian. . . . I remember."

"Yes; and I can do it."

"Supposing you can do it—taking you at your own valuation, what do you think your knowledge is worth?"

"You shall see what I can do, first. It is no secret, and if any one else can do it, let them. I experimented in Germany, on English iron, and no one except myself could do it."

"Is it no secret? Is it only the old dodge of putting in the manganese? Then, Armstrong, I think very little of your secret. Everybody knows it."

"Do they know how much manganese to put in? Do they know the right time? Can they make it a certainty?"

"No."

"I can, Mr. Bayliss," Jack said, with a quiet air of assurance. "I am going to make you an offer, subject to my doing what I pretend to do."

"Go on."

"My power, if it exists, will give the foundry, when it is exercised, a strength that no other works can hope for . . . will it not?"

"Ay."

"If you had the use of it, you could increase your power and name, and therefore your influence and position, to say nothing of your income, which is perhaps great enough already."

"No man's income is great enough. I made a hundred thousand last year, but I am not satisfied even with that."

"I should help you to make more. These are my terms. You will give me a despotic control over the furnaces, always provided that I fulfil my promise to turn you out steel as good as any that can be made in Germany, and from Spanish as well as English iron— so long you will give me such a share in the business as shall guarantee me an income at least——"

He named boldly a very large sum.

Mr. Bayliss looked at him with admiration.

"And if I refuse?"

"Then I go to Captain Perrymont. If he refuses I go to London, and start a company which will build a foundry here."

"You young viper!" Mr. Bayliss replied. "Would you bite the hand that nursed you?"

Jack laughed.

"I have been brought up in your works, Mr. Bayliss. It is a hard school. I mean to be rich. I am grateful to you for a good many things, but chiefly for the lesson that a man who likes to push himself on can get on. I am one who pushes. My father, from all I understand, was one who was pushed."

"Ay," said Bayliss, "you are right there. Johnny was a good deal pushed. . . . When do you want to make your experiments?"

"When you please. . . . Now . . . if you please."

Not that day only, but several days afterwards, Jack experimented in the foundry. He was within the truth when he boasted of the possession of an invaluable power. He had watched the molten metal so long that he knew every mood, so to speak, of the iron, and could read it as no one else could. Everybody knew that to improve the English steel the addition of manganese was necessary. What nobody knew except Jack was the quantity, varying with the quality of the metal, that had to be put in, and the time to put it in. And he knew it. Therefore he was invaluable. For if you put in too much, or too little, or at the wrong time, you spoil the whole.

Bayliss and his foreman Hodder watched and inspected. There was no secret, as Jack told them, only he was the only man in the world who could do it.

" What do you think, Hodder ? "

" Well, sir, if I might be so bold, I should say—take him at his own price, and it will be a cheap bargain."

CHAPTER XVII.

"Come over and see me. I cannot believe that you are as cruel and as false as you profess to be. Come and tell me so once more, before I act. Or come and tell me that it is all a horrid dream, and that you are still my own Jack, as I am still your own loving and most miserable Adelaide."

This was the letter which was handed to Jack by Keziah, who accosted him on his way home.

"Here's a letter for you, Mr. Armstrong," she said.

He took it, and read it under a gas-lamp. Then he tore the missive into small pieces and gave them back to her.

"That is my answer—the only answer I

have to give her except this. Tell her that she may act as she thinks proper. I have nothing else to say. Good-night to you, Mrs. Bastable."

The woman received the fragments, and solemnly deposited them in a capacious side pocket.

"Don't say good-night, Jack Armstrong," she whispered, looking furtively across the road. "Stay and have a word or two with me."

"I have nothing to say to you."

"No; but I have a good deal to say to you, Jack Armstrong. It isn't that I knew you when you were a little boy, and had you in the house, and kissed you a dozen times a day, pretty little boy that you were. That's nothing, because I didn't even know your name, nor who was your father. Lord! if I had known."

"Well, Mrs. Bastable, and if you had known."

"I always loved you, even then. And if you'll believe me, a middle-aged respectable deserted wife, I love you still. And I'd help you, if I could."

"But I am afraid you cannot."

"I could, and I would. I told Miss Norah that I would, only I want you to tell me what *she's* done." This, with a jerk of the head in the direction of Laburnum Villa, to signify that it was Mrs. Merrion she meant.

"You live with her," said Jack. "You learn her secrets, I suppose. Why do you want to ask me anything?"

"She's not a good lot, my cousin Jenny," said Mrs. Bastable. "And she keeps her secrets mostly to herself."

"Your cousin — Jenny? Who is your cousin Jenny?"

"There . . . there . . . my poor tongue . . . I mean Mrs. Merrion, of course— Adelaide."

"Oh!"

"That is, she calls herself Adelaide. Jack Armstrong, don't tell her I told you; but her name's Jenny, as Miss Norah knows already. Jenny she was christened, and Jenny she'll die, whatever she calls herself. Now, then, tell me all about it."

Jack looked at her.

"If you know what you profess to know, you

ought to be able to tell me something. I've got nothing to tell you, except that I was a young fool, and she made me think I was in love with her."

"She always does. She makes all the men in love with her. She's made more fools than any woman of her age in the world. Bless you, is that all?"

"But she's got letters of mine."

"She's got letters from dozens. Lord! you're only one fool among many—the biggest fool, perhaps, because you've fallen in love with a woman old enough to be your mother, when there's lots of young girls in Esbrough as would jump at you. For shame, Jack Armstrong! When your father fell in love, it was with a handsome young wench like me— as I was then—or else with a sweet pretty lady like your poor mother."

"A fool I was, no doubt," said Jack. "And now I know it."

"Don't be afraid, Jack Armstrong. Don't mind what she says. She barks, but she don't dare bite. There's them behind as holds her back. As for letters, she's got letters from Mr. Bayliss, and from Captain Perrymont, and

. . . and . . . all the old fools in the place. What's she to do with your letters?"

This was comfort to Jack.

"Can you get her to give them back?" he asked.

"No, I can't. She locks them all up in her davenport, and there they are. She won't give them back for all my asking. Jack, have nothing more to say to her, and don't be afraid of her. She shan't harm you, whatever mischief she does."

"Mr. Bayliss? Captain Perrymont? Do you mean that they write to her?"

"Captain Perrymont hasn't written for a month and more. I think he's broke off. Mr. Bayliss always comes himself, regular, once a week."

"Good heavens! She told me she had never seen him even, and did not know him by sight."

"Jenny and lies means much the same thing," said Mr. Bastable, "though she *is* my cousin."

"And who was General Merrion?"

Mrs. Bastable looked round again. Then she whispered in his ear, hoarsely,

"There never was no General Merrion."

"No General Merrion?"

"She never had a husband at all. She's a single woman."

"Then," said Jack, coolly, "she's a considerably more artful woman than I took her for. Suppose, Mrs. Bastable, suppose she was to bring an action against me, would you be prepared to prove this in the witness-box?"

"I'd prove that, and plenty more, if she tries to harm you. And I've told her so, only she won't believe it. Ah! she's a wilful woman, a wicked woman."

"Then why do you live with her?"

"Because I can't help it. Because I'm tied to her. Because I'm the only person in the world that cares for her and isn't afraid of her. And because I mind the old days when Jenny was a pretty young slip of a thing, good and innocent, and thought of nothing but a bit of ribbon or some coloured rag to set off her beauty. Ah! you gentlemen, you think we women haven't got any hearts. What does it matter to me that Jenny hasn't turned out so quiet and good as the rest of the family? Blood's thicker than water; and I mean to look after her, if all the world gives her up."

"I believe you're a kind-hearted woman," said Jack. "And now I'll tell you something about it. I was only eighteen, and she turned my brain. One night, after I'd been telling her that I loved her and all the rest of the nonsense, she got me to write her a promise of marriage. She wrote it, and I signed it. I would have signed anything, then. Then Norah came, and I saw what a fool I had been. All day long, you see, I was at work and thinking of my work; and in the evening she made a fool of me."

"Same as she does to all of them. Lord! what creatures men are, to be sure. Made a fool of you, indeed! Why couldn't you fall in love with Miss Bayliss, now, if you wanted a pretty girl?"

"I don't know."

"Well, I'm glad you didn't. You've got a sweet girl and a lovely girl, now: and if you are not kind to her, Jack Armstrong, I'll never forgive you as sure as my name's Keziah Bastable."

"Of course, I shall be kind to Norah," he replied.

"Ah! there's different sorts of kindnesses. I've known men that were kind to their wives who'd beat them with sticks if they got into a rage."

"My good soul, be rational."

"And their wives loved them all the same, poor bleeding lambs! I've known men who were kind to their wives, but never asked themselves if the poor things were happy, nor what they wanted, and saw them pine away for want of a little thought. And I've known men who were kind to their wives, or said they were, when they'd given them a comfortable house, and left them alone by themselves the long day, and sometimes the long night. Don't you do that, Jack Armstrong. You're masterful and she's loving; you're strong and she's trustful. You've won away her heart, poor thing, and she believes you're an angel from heaven. Think of her after you've married her, Jack Armstrong. Think of the wife that wants to tell you everything, and to put all her thoughts into your heart, and don't be wrapped up for ever in your wheels and your engines. It wasn't for nothing that you were born in a foundry, when the furnace was roaring and the engine blowing and the chimneys smoking. I was there, and the first thing as ever you did was to stretch out your tiny fist to the fire and clutch at it. And the doctor says: 'Let's have a look at this son of Vulcan?' I said then, for I was a prophet before I was a witch and had familiar sperruts, I said: 'It's a great man he's going to be, give him the chance.' A beautiful baby you were, much too beautiful to live. But don't be carried away with your cleverness, Jack. Don't neglect your wife to make a little money. Have faith, and give her your evenings at least, and let her thoughts be your thoughts. I am but a foolish woman, and a sinful witch and a clairvoyong, but I can't bear to think of your father's son doing anything but what's right."

She seized his hand and held it for a moment. The tears were running down her homely cheeks, but his big bright eyes looked at her full, with an intentness which brought back the days when he was a boy, and she stood transformed, waiting for the silent summons to the mesmeric room.

Then she left him: but returned again in a moment.

"I've got something more on my mind. Let me talk to you to-morrow. Now I must get back to Jenny. It's the time when she wants her brandy and water."

Jack went home. In Norah's room were only herself and Myles, for "the boy" had been sent to bed. Myles was silent and subdued, as he had been for some months, since, in fact, his disappointing tour in the provinces.

Jack sat down between them fronting the fire. Norah was on the right, a book in her hands, but not reading, and Myles on the left nursing his knee and gazing into the coals.

And so all three were silent. Norah lifting a corner of her eyes to Jack when he was sitting near her, his foot actually touching her dress, a mode of personal contact which, distant as it was, refreshed her soul.

"Myles," said Jack, after a long pause, "we are very silent to-night."

"We are, Jack. Norah, alaunah, 'tis dull you'll be."

She shook her head.

"Myles, do you remember how you used to tell us stories, Norah and me, in the old days?

There was Pettigo and Ennis fair, and Connemara wakes, and Connaught fights. Do you ever think of them, now?"

"Never, Jack; 'twas in the ould bad days. Norah knows all about it. I tould her myself."

"I've forgotten, father," said Norah.

"So have I, Myles," said Jack. "It was not to bring them up in your mind that I asked if you remembered the stories. Only I thought I would tell you one, if you would like to hear it."

"Sure I would," said Myles languidly, "if Norah would."

Jack looked at her and began clearing his throat.

"About a thousand years ago, or it may be two thousand, because the books have got confused and so the dates are all as wrong as the repealer's facts."

"Jack, ye're takin' advantage," said Myles, waking up.

"Well, then, it doesn't matter how long ago. But there were once a girl and a boy. The boy's name was John, but they called him Jack."

"Aha!" cried Myles, revived and alert. "May I have my pipe in here, Norah asthore? That's my dear girl. And now, Jack, the story. The colleen's name was Norah."

"Of course."

"Av course. When ye're done blushin', my princess of Pettigo, where you ought to have been born, give me a shavin' of paper for a pipelight. Go on, Jack, 'tis a mighty fine story."

"They were brought up by a kind-hearted man, who was the girl's father."

"He was a dhrunken scoundrel," said Myles. "I knew him well. That is, I didn't, but my great-great-grandfather fifty hundred times removed, who was then the king of Ennis, often said he'd live to be hanged."

"His Majesty was not always a prophet to be depended on," said Jack. "Well, things happened so that after the little maid was five years old and the boy was nine, or thereabouts, this good man had to give them up, in order to get them educated. The girl went off to stay with a Saxon princess, not so beautiful as she was good——"

"Thrue, Jack, gospel thrue."

"And the boy with a priest who wore a white robe on Sundays and read books all the week, and was the best man that ever lived. Don't interrupt, Myles. Well, the boy, a selfish, conceited young dog, took to reading books too, and was never so happy as when he was reading books and learning to make things out of iron and steel. And he never, or hardly ever, gave a thought to the little maid at all."

"Oh! Jack," said Norah.

"A more selfish boy never lived. Meantime, the little girl was growing up too. She grew up so beautiful that everybody fell in love with her, and the angels were jealous of her."

Myles took his pipe out of his mouth, and with the courtesy of a Castilian, stepped across the hearthrug, just one short step and a bit, and kissed his daughter's hand.

"I'd like to see the angel that could come up to her," he said, resuming his seat with a smile of blissful content. "Go on, Jack, 'tis a beautiful story."

"The angels were jealous of her," Jack repeated.

"Don't, Jack," Norah murmured.

"When she sang, it was like playing on the strings of your heart."

"It was, it was," said Myles.

"And when she spoke it was like music. Her hair was black and she had dark blue eyes, so dark as to look almost black, at first."

"Jack, I forbid you to go on with your description," cried Norah, blushing again.

"If you have no story to follow, I will get up and go to bed."

"Wait—I am coming to the story. The girl became a woman, and everybody said she was fit to be a queen——"

"Jack!"

"And what was better, she had never forgotten the boy she used to play with. Every year when her father came to see her, she used to ask after Jack; and all the year round, she used to think about him; he all the time never thinking about her at all."

"That was because he was learning to make himself clever," said Norah, "and had something else to do."

"Don't go beyond the story, Norah. Well, the boy became a young man and went to live with Myles, little Norah's father, and worked in the king's foundries, where he made machines and engines and all sorts of wonderful things, and thought at first about nothing but getting rich. But he made the acquaintance of a lady who was dressed in velvets and silks, and who called herself a princess, though she was nothing, really, but a common kitchen maid, as every true princess would see at a glance; but she was clever, and knew how to deceive people and make them think that they were in love with her."

Then Myles turned very red. But Norah didn't notice him, because she was looking shyly at Jack, and she was trembling.

"She got hold of the young man when he was only eighteen, and used to make him sit with her of an evening. She played to him, and sang to him, gave him delicate little dinners dressed daintily for him, and one night, when they were all alone, she made him sit at her feet and say he loved her."

"She's a witch," groaned Myles.

"Then she made him write her letters. Not one letter, but hundreds, in which the boy, who knew hardly any other woman, told her over and over again all his fancied love."

"Poor Jack!" said Myles.

"So it went on, and nothing happened for a time. Then the colleen came home to her father; and at sight of her and at speech with her, the foolish fancy flew out of that young man's heart like a dream of the night. He feared that all his imagined love was a delusion, and that the woman, the pretended princess, could be nothing in the world to him. He told her so. She laughed at him, told him that it was a passing whim, and dared him to break it off. So he was afraid. But then, bit by bit, he saw, talking to the colleen every day, what true love meant; he saw what a woman should be, and what life might be made with such a woman by his side. And then, overpowered by passion, one day, Myles, he did what he ought not to have done—he told the girl, the Princess Norah, that he loved her, but that he was engaged to another woman."

"Hush, Norah, hush, my pretty," cried Myles, holding the girl to his heart, as she half stepped, half knelt across to him, and fell into his arms. "Don't cry, alaunah. Sure, 'tis the most beautiful story that ever I heard. Go on, Jack, and more power to your elbow."

"Then he went away. While he was abroad, his heart was full of Norah. He thought about her every day and all the night. He learned to loathe the name of the other woman. He came home, and a second time he told his Norah all the sad story. Then he went to the other woman and told her. Again she laughed in his face, tried to cajole him, and then she threatened him. He left her at last, declaring that, do what she might, he would never set foot in her house again."

"And then, Jack?" asked Myles.

"That's all, Myles," he said. "Forgive me, and tell us that we may love one another."

Myles did not answer, but the tears came into his eyes and trickled down his seamed and worn cheeks. Norah stayed where she was. Presently he raised her, and taking her hand, laid it in the great brown fist that belonged to Jack.

"Whom should she marry but you, Jack?

would she be my own daughter, my Norah, if she did not love you better than herself?"

And then, with great presence of mind, Myles left them together.

CHAPTER XVIII.

"I OFFER you, Armstrong, a handsome salary, dependent on results," said Mr. Bayliss, in his own private office, "but no partnership. You shall work this power of yours to my advantage, and no other's. That is my offer."

"Then I refuse it," said Jack.

"Very well. Go now, and see what Perrymont will do."

"That is what I intend to do."

"I took this boy," said Bayliss, putting his hands into his pockets, and looking ahead as if he were addressing posterity, "when he had not a penny and knew nothing. I trained him. I gave him employment. I taught him his trade. And now I offer him a handsome salary—a handsome salary. He turns upon me, like the worm, and goes to Perrymont."

"It is true that you took me as a boy," said Jack, " and for nothing. It is also true that if my father were living, he would be your partner still, and you would be only half as rich as you are now."

A random shot, but it hit between wind and water. Bayliss changed colour.

"I had nothing to do with might-have-beens. I am a practical man. I have had small opportunities, and I have had great ones. But I never let one slip. You, Armstrong, are one of my small ones."

"On the contrary," said Jack, "I am one of your great ones."

"Are you here to bully me, or am I here——"

"To bully me? Neither, Mr. Bayliss. I am here having proved myself the possessor of a power that will make me rich. You offer to make me a servant. I will not be a servant. I intend to be a master. If not a master in your works, then in other's. You know that I am not friendless."

"You may go to Perrymont," said Bayliss. "Come back if you like, when you have seen him. My offer is still open. Oh! there is one other thing. Your eccentric friend, Mr. Myles Cuolahan."

"Your old associate, in old days."

"That is an infernal lie, if he said so," burst out the *parvenu*. "I say it is an infernal lie. Tell him I said so."

"I think I had better not. It is the truth, and you know it. He was an associate of yourself and of my father, when you all drank together, and were proud of being the friends of the last Armstrong left in Esbrough, poor though he was."

"We are proud of our family, then, among other things. Jack Armstrong, you will eventually bring yourself to the devil."

"Perhaps. Good evening, Mr. Bayliss."

Bayliss, left alone, began with the marvellous rapidity which was his strong point, to make estimates and plans. "He would bring thirty thousand a year to the concern. Would it be worth while to let him have his terms? Son of my old partner. Esbrough will never forget that. How the old things strike and crop up again—crop up again." He fidgeted in his chair. "Bah! as if anything would hurt me that might crop up. There are those papers at the banker's. They have had them for fifteen years. I will fetch them out, and destroy them. Then, if they are asked for, I can say that they are lost and the Bank knows that they were once in existence. I will burn them all. Fool that I was! And yet, the safety of it. And it was the making of me."

When a certain fear came over him his form seemed to shrink, and his full round face suddenly became crossed with dimples.

"It was the making of me. They wanted to know if I was a responsible man. I showed them the papers. The land was mine by deed of transfer, signed, witnessed and all; signed by me, witnessed by the old clerk Kislingbury, dead and comfortably out of the way, and the fellow Bastable, the rogue whom I sent away—abroad. He has never come back since. The land was mine, and the vein was mine; all the rest was easy. Paul Bayliss, my boy, such acts are like rebellions. If they are successful, they are great strokes of policy. If they fail, they are great crimes. Mine has not failed. It has prospered. I defy the Fates to do me any harm. To-morrow

I get the papers out of the Bank, and I destroy them. There are no copies. Who can swear to a forge—to a signature when there is no signature to swear to? And if my word is not as good as Bastable's, even if he is living, which is not likely, what is the world coming to? Paul Bayliss is a millionaire. Paul Bayliss is a justice of the peace. Paul Bayliss shall be a Baronet, before he is done. Baronet? By Gad, he shall be a Baron—first Lord Esbrough, and shall pass his title on through his daughter to his grandchildren. Men must take their opportunities, or must make them."

Here a knock came to the door. It was Hodder.

"I beg your pardon, sir. Can I have five minutes?"

Mr. Bayliss, who had been walking up and down the room with his great shock of brown hair a good deal dishevelled, ran his fingers through it, and instantly assumed his magisterial air.

"I was making a few troublesome calculations, Hodder. But go on—go on. What is it?"

"I am afraid, sir, that I have discovered a bad business."

Mr. Bayliss took out his watch.

"Five minutes only. Come to the point."

"Smith has forged a cheque."

"Forged a cheque? Do you mean to tell me that an *employé* of mine has forged—actually forged—a cheque?"

He filled himself out and puffed his cheeks, like an offended turkey cock.

"I am sure of it," said Hodder.

He gave him a paper.

"That is not my signature, and a clumsy imitation. Hodder, it is a wicked world. I had confidence in Smith. Was not his salary increased last January?"

"It was, sir. Ten pounds."

Bayliss looked at him, and at the cheque.

"Ten pounds. We try to help them who work for us, Hodder, and this is our reward. This is . . . our . . . reward. Well, . . . well."

Hodder began to stammer.

"I brought it to you, sir, at once."

"Of course."

"And . . . and . . . if I might speak a word for the poor fellow."

"Speak, Hodder." Mr. Bayliss seated himself. "I am a magistrate, but forget that. Say all you can."

"He is recently married. His wife is ill. He thought, perhaps, that he could replace the amount, or get a real cheque, or something. He is in dreadful misery of mind. If you would only pass it over."

"Hodder, how many men have I got in my employ?"

"I don't know, sir, within fifty or so."

"There are many hundreds, at least, as you *do* know. I should think your zeal in my service might have led you to know accurately how many there are, if only to show the importance of the works. But let that pass. If we let this one wrong act go unpunished, it will be an inducement to others to do the same. A. B. is hard up—A. B. steals. We are to have pity on A. B. No, Hodder. I am sorry—I am more than sorry. Smith has a wife, and he belongs to a respectable family. It will be a bitter blow to them, but it is a blow that must be dealt in mercy to the others. Let every one on these works, on Paul Bayliss's works know, that if he is in distress he may come to the master. But if he steals, the law must take its course. Forgery! And on MY works."

Hodder was silent. This was grandeur.

"Prosecute, Hodder. Put the thing out of my hands at once. I am a witness, I suppose, because this signature is mine. You have spoiled my dinner, Hodder."

Hodder went out. In his own office was a young man, little more than a boy, with white face and trembling limbs. "It won't do, Smith," said Hodder. "Damn him! He is as hard as nails. We are to prosecute."

"Oh! my poor wife," groaned the miserable forger. "Who will tell her?"

"There's a chance," whispered Hodder. "Take the train to Hull. Take the steamer —one of our own iron steamers—to Spain. It goes to-night. Then you can get across somehow, to South America. They won't look for you. When you are there, with an assumed name, write to me *here*, when no one will suspect, and I will send you your wife. Get away quietly, and I will give you four and twenty hours' start, and tell your wife something that will put her off the scent. I'm not a rich man, but here is something to help you as far as Spain. You may get a passage for nothing, if you make out that you are going for the firm, but don't try it on if you can help it."

"God bless you for ever!" cried the man. "And you will not tell my wife all?"

"Nothing. Only, if there is a row, we will make her believe that your man did it. Now, write her a line quick, and be off."

At five o'clock, Hodder presented himself again to his employer.

"Have you got a warrant out for Smith's business, sir?"

"I thought it was your business, Hodder. Well, get one at once."

"Yes, sir, as soon as I can. I suppose to-morrow will be time enough for the arrest."

"Well, when Smith comes to-morrow he will be met by what he little expects."

Hodder sighed.

"Yes, sir. If every one had his deserts——"

"What the devil do you mean, Hodder?"

Bayliss faced him with an expression so savage that the foreman only stammered, and walked out.

When, next morning, it was discovered that Smith was missing, Bayliss heard the news from Hodder, and told him to institute a search. But as Hodder did nothing, and as other events occurred, Smith got off free. In fact, a few months later, Smith returned to Esbrough, after a visit to Paraguay, and took away his wife, bearing still, so to speak, his sword. The moral of which is, not that you are to forge a cheque when you are hard up, dear young friend starting in life, because that is wicked; nor is it that you are to help the wicked man to turn away from the consequences of his wickedness, because that is compounding of felony; nor that you are to let off your servants when they err and trespass, because that is the weakness of generosity; but it is . . . "He may run who reads," and we will not spoil the story by adding the moral.

Jack went to Captain Perrymont. The Captain heard him at full length.

"I see your drift, my boy," he said. "I should like to help you because you are an Armstrong. But I cannot, because I have made up my mind to have nothing to do with new things. I am rich enough, and so is my son. The devil of it is that we can't help getting richer. Where the fortunes of the Perrymonts and Baylisses will end, Lord knows. I'm ashamed to see the money pouring in, and we not knowing what to do with it."

"Well, sir. Then you will have nothing to say to me."

"Everything to say to you. I like you. Frank likes you. Come and dine as often as you please, and the oftener the better. But I won't make myself richer by your means."

Jack went away as sad as the young man who was bidden to sell all he had.

He had got a great thing: a power which no other man possessed, he looked to it for the establishment of his own fortune with all the collateral issues that a generous and unselfish man could see springing thereform. He had returned with a sudden confidence and exultation. And this was the result: Paul Bayliss would make him a servant, and Captain Perrymont would have nothing to do with him at all. The inventor who has worked out an idea that no one will back up, though it would regenerate civilisation; the young fellow who has got a carpet bag full of poems which no one will publish; the novelist who has a romance that no one will buy; the dramatist who has a play that no one will act; the disappointment of all these together would not make up that which filled poor Jack's breast as he left Perrymont and walked quietly away.

People met him and shook hands. Frank Perrymont shouted to him across the street; he mechanically answered, and passed on. That morning he had been a rich man, able to marry his Norah. He was now a poor man. That morning he had been successful. He was now ruined. Presently there met him Mr. Bayliss himself—he walking slowly down the street, looking out, in fact, for Jack's return.

He beckoned him.

"Well, Armstrong, what says Perrymont?"

"He says . . . . in fact, he will have nothing to do with me."

"Good. Now, I make you my offer over again."

"And I refuse it. I will be no mere servant.'

"You talked of setting up a Company here. You can try, of course. But see what they would say in London of a Company in opposition to Paul Bayliss."

"I can wait," said Jack. "But I will work my power yet, and from my own hand, too."

"Try to work it here, my young Jack, and you will have Paul Bayliss against you at every turn. There is not a man in all this place that does not belong to me somehow or other. Look at that man across the street. You see how he takes off his hat to me. He owes me nothing. I have never given him a penny. Yet he is obsequious, because I could, if I pleased, smash him. I could smash them all if I liked. Those who get in my way I do smash. If you get in my way I smash you. Remember, that in Esbrough I am king, and I mean to be king. You may be one of my subjects, and if you do your duty you will be paid for it. I rule here. And now make war with me if you dare."

He strode off, puffing his cheeks like some infuriated bubbly jock in a stable yard, leaving Jack on the curbstone, half amused and half savage. Scrape the rust off the man who has "made himself" manners as well as money, and you find, below, the man as he was before he was made. Paul Bayliss was as coarse, as self-seeking, as vulgar, in these days of splendour, as when he was the beggarly partner in a ruinous scrap iron factory, and got drunk whenever he could spare five shillings or borrow that sum from poor Johnny Armstrong.

"War!" said Jack. "Well, let us have war. I will go and see Mr. Fortescue. Perhaps, after all, he is too big for me."

Then the humorous side of the thing seized him, and he went home laughing as he walked, so that the sentimental girls who met him thought their Jack was frivolous, and all the frivolous girls thought their Jack was charming. For among the women of all classes and all ages, from Ella, ruling sovereign of beauty, to the humble factory girl, there was unanimity of opinion—Jack Armstrong was the production of which Esbrough might chiefly boast; and Jack was, so far as was known, free, Norah Cuolahan being, presumably, a sister only. It was true that he went to Mrs. Merrion's, but so did a good many people. And she was old enough to be his mother.

"There goes Jack Armstrong."

"I like him best when he is meditating in church," said Ethel the pensive, "his noble brow is marble white. Did you ever see him smile? Oh—h! It makes you understand the curving lips that the novelists talk about."

"I like him best," said Fanny the flirt, "when he's laughing and talking. Did you ever waltz with him? Oh—h! It makes you understand being held up tight, like Ouida talks about."

"There goes Jack Armstrong!"

"I call that a man, girls," said Poll, one of the hands. "He don't fool about. He works like a man, and he fights like a man; and he treats a pretty girl like a man. Lord! he's chucked me under the chin a dozen times. Glad to see you back again, Handsome Jack."

"How are you, Poll? How are you all, girls?" answered Jack, at the same time taking off his hat to Ethel and Fanny.

CHAPTER XIX.

"But you have lost nothing, Jack," said Norah, anxious to find the rosy side. "You have escaped the clutches of a greedy man. That is all."

"I wish it were all. What the greedy man, as you call him, says is true. He is absolute master in this place. No company, unless it were far stronger than any I could get together, would dare to work here in the teeth of Paul Bayliss. He is King Paul, Emperor Paul, Pope Paul, in Esbrough."

"There are other places besides Esbrough, Jack."

"Not for me, Norah. You know my history. It came upon me like some great gift from heaven—the knowledge that I belonged to a once honourable race. This place is full of Armstrongs: the church holds their bones;

and the old people here look upon me with respect because I am an Armstrong, so that the desire has grown upon me to be a leader in this town and no other. I seem to belong to the very soil of the town. I want to make the old name rise again."

"And you will, Jack—you will," said the girl. "But, oh! Jack, if you are to be a great man, how can you love me who have no family traditions to help you out?"

"My love, are you not the Countess of Connaught? Don't we know all about the ancient kings from whom the Cuolahans, and the MacSwires, and the MacBriartys, and the MacSwineys, your cousins, are all descended?"

Norah laughed. It was only a suburb of a new city, with little villas, spick-and-span, their fronts smeared with the smoke of the factories, their gardens encrusted with the soot, the air dank with smoke and fume. What a place to talk of kings and great families!

"You love me, Jack. That is enough. I will be nothing more, and we will have no questions. Take me back now, for my father will be wanting me to talk to him. Is he not improved, Jack?"

"Myles is a gentleman, Norah, and a nobleman born. He condescends to collect rents. When I was a boy, he was the grandest of men to me, the kindest and the strongest. You ought to have seen him fight Patsy MacNulty."

"Don't, Jack."

"I won't, Norah. But you have no reason to be ashamed of your father. Go back now, and send your boy to bed. He is getting feeble, that boy, and I fear he will not arrive at years of discretion. I will join you presently."

But Norah saw no more of Jack that evening. For when he left her at the gate, and pulled out a short wooden pipe to help him through half an hour's silent colloquy alone with himself, he became aware of a woman watching him. Jack did not like being watched. It was not the first time that the uneasy feeling had crossed his mind that some one was hunting him down. So he went up to the woman and confronted her.

"Mrs. Bastable?" for it was that worthy lady, "if you've got any message for me from your cousin Jenny, or Adelaide, or

Pamela, or whatever she chooses to call herself, you may go away without giving it. For she may do her—I mean, she may do whatever she likes, and I will fight her."

"I've got no message, Mr. Armstrong," said the woman, humbly. "It isn't that, at all, Jack Armstrong. But I do want to help you."

"Thank you, Mrs. Bastable, very much. I do not see how you can, but I'm grateful all the same."

"Perhaps I may. Look, Jack," she laid her hand on his arm. "Lord! How like you are to your father. It was fields here, then, all the blessed fields, and no screeching engines, when we used to walk here, him and me, his arm round my neck, and me thinking he meant something. But of course it was only a young gentleman's play. What are we poor girls for in the world, but to please the men? And who is so happy as a girl that pleases a gentleman? He meant to amuse himself, Johnny Armstrong, and I—well, I cried and was unhappy when he married. And if you'll believe a sinful woman who's had familiar sperruts by the twenty, I never loved Bastable a patch upon Johnny Armstrong."

"What has all that got to do with it, my good soul? Had we not better forget the past?"

"'Tis my past," she said, simply, "not yours. No, Jack, I can't forget, nor never could, when I was an innocent young girl, and loved the dearest man in the world. Not that he destroyed my innocence, don't think that. Poor Johnny was a good man and soft-hearted, even when the drink was in him. He was not like Bastable, the villain, with his mesmerizing and clairvoynging, and sperrut-rapping. Ah! dear—dear—dear!"

"Would you mind, Mrs. Bastable, coming to the point?"

She sighed heavily.

"You want to get back to that sweet girl, Jack Armstrong. Well, you are like your father. He never could bear to be long away when he was in love. Good love, too; fierce love, passionate love, that made your heart go quicker, and your head reel when his strong arm caught your waist, and his kisses came like a hailstorm all over your face. I never saw the like. Girls like it, Jack. Don't be afraid when she wants you to leave off. Let her have all that is in your heart, and God bless her for a happy woman."

"You said," Jack returned, calmly, "that you wanted to do me some service."

"Anything, Jack Armstrong. The smallest and the greatest. Now listen: It's your letters. Suppose I get those letters for you. I know where they are. Suppose I take them when she is asleep."

Jack shook his head.

"That can't be thought of. I gave them to her, and she must send them back to me of her own free will."

"Men are such noodles," said his friend. "Well, have it your own way, Jack. Do you know when Paul Bayliss bought your father's last bit of land?"

"No, I do not."

"It was the only thing left to him: that and the partnership that Bayliss got into his own hands. Only the day before he died, just one day, I met him: 'Johnny,' I said, for old friendship's sake, 'you're going on bad.' 'I am, Keziah,' he said. 'Then,' said

I, 'why don't you reform, Johnny?' 'It's too late,' he said. 'Everything is gone, all but the field by the sea, and that would go too, but that I'm determined to leave the child unborn something. He shan't say, if it's a boy, that I stripped him of everything. It's only a forty acre lot and poor land, but it's the last bit left of all the Armstrongs' property. And it has only a little mortgage on it.' Then he left me, and the next day he was a corpse, if you can rightly call a corpse what was only a pile of white ash. But I remember his words as if it was yesterday."

Jack looked at her attentively.

"Once," she went on, "six months after he was dead, and before Bastable and I went up to London, I met Paul Bayliss and asked him where you were gone. 'Put out to nurse,' says he, 'and comfortably looked after.' 'The boy's got something,' I said. 'What something?' he says. 'The field next to Squire Perrymont's One Tree meadow,' I said. 'You're a fool,' he says, and he changed all colours. Now, from that day to this he's never set eyes on me. I've been five years in this place, but Paul Bayliss does not know

I am in the town at all, and wouldn't know me if he saw me; for, and it's a dreadful thing to think of, there's nothing in the world, not a dozen babies even, drags and tears a woman's good looks to pieces like having to do with familiar sperruts. Mesmerizing is bad, and clairvoyonging makes you pale, but the sperruts it is which pull a woman down and makes her old before her time. And me only forty-eight."

"Are you quite sure of what you say, Mrs. Bastable?" asked Jack.

"I remember it all as if it was yesterday. It was fixed in my memory by that awful night when you were born, and by the look that Paul Bayliss gave me when he said, 'You're a fool, Keziah Bastable.'"

"Can you keep a secret, my good woman?"

She smiled superior.

"I'm full of secrets. There's some secrets I can't let out if I was to try. Yours are that kind of secret. There's some I can't keep in. Jenny's are that kind. Don't ask me anything about poor Jenny, else I shall tell all out and disgrace the family. But tear me with pincers and pull off my flesh with red-hot tongs, as Bastable used to threaten when I wouldn't call up Peter, and you won't get anything out of me about yourself."

"Then promise to hold your tongue till I let you speak."

Jack left her, and instead of going home, strode off down town.

The forty acre field close to Captain Perrymont's One Tree meadow! It was there that the iron was found. That vein, the richest of all, richer than any in the Ravendale county, which ran straight under the sea, to be worked for miles, was in his father's ground. He had long known that. And his father, the day before he died, had declared it to be still his. If that were true—if that were true—but then it rested on the word of a silly woman. How should she know? The works were built upon it, with money that came out of it; half the fortune that Bayliss owned, at least, came from it; it was the beginning of his wonderful luck. How if—and here he paused and grew pale, looking about as if he were thinking an unworthy thing—how if Paul Bayliss had claimed the land by some fraud, by some statement that was not true?

The power of reputation is great. This huge Colossus so grandly strode across the town of Esbrough, which lived under his shadow, seeing no sunshine, so to speak, save what was reflected from his burnished legs, that Jack trembled as he thought that, after all, this gigantic idol might have feet of clay, like him in the prophet's vision.

"And if . . ." he thought—"if it should be so; if I can force him to prove his title. He offered peace or war. What if I give him war, in a quarter where he least expects it?"

He bethought him of a young lawyer, a man of his own age, with whom he had some kind of acquaintance, made upon the cricket field, and resolved to communicate the story and ask his advice.

The young man learned in all the crafts and subtleties of the devil was at home, alone, gloomy, with a pipe from which he strove to draw solace. Before him was a pile of letters, chiefly bills, and around him, for he sat in the same room which served him for office during the day, was an emptiness of tin boxes, a vacuity of shelves, an absence of parchments, which bespoke the scanty *clientèle*.

"Armstrong? Of all men in the world, I least expected you. Come in. Come in. I can offer you—no, there's only beer. But you can have that, and help me to swear at the world."

"I come on business, Clifton. I want your opinion on a long story."

"Welcome is the man who comes to have a talk with me in this cursed town. Thrice welcome he who comes to talk business. Now then."

* * * * *

"I hate Bayliss," said the lawyer. "That has nothing to do with the legal issues, but it shows that I will give you all the help I can. If he had been born ten thousand years ago, he would have done what the gentleman in the classical story did, made a bridge of iron and a chariot of brass, and driven across, thinking he was Jupiter himself. By Gad! he *has* made the bridge of iron already, and we must, in common Christian charity, try to prevent him making the other thing. However, let us see."

He went on muttering and talking.

" You are two and twenty. That is against

us, because he has held for more than twenty years undisturbed, but if we can prove that he took the field and used it as his own, knowing that you were alive, and held it, letting the world know it . . . we might make it unpleasant for the red-faced Jupiter.

"Or if we could force him to show his title-deeds, and he had none, we might make this bloated Crœsus wish he had never been born.

"And, if we do anything rash, Jack Armstrong, he will be down upon you and me like one of his own steam hammers. As for me, I am smashed already; but I should not like you to be smashed as well."

"Never mind me. Think it over, and give me your advice."

"It's a queer business, Jack. I believe you will turn out to be the original Jack the Giant Killer. Your boots—no, they appear to be not unlike my own. The bean, is that planted? Is the old woman frightened? . . . The fact is, my dear boy, that I am so taken aback with the trembling delight of attacking this great big bloated porpoise, that I feel like a girl going to be married, or like a boy going into the sea for the first bathe of the year, or a soldier going into a battle. We may want money. Have you got any?"

"None of my own. If we have a case, I could get money."

"I do not think we shall want it. The question is, how he got that field. Land doesn't change hands like shillings. If a man gets a meadow he gets a bit of paper with it. Your father died suddenly, and nobody took the trouble to look into his affairs. Mr. Bayliss allowed you to be carried off anywhere. That is fishy. Then he never inquired after you; that is fishy again, considering you were his partner's son. When he made your acquaintance again, after an interval of sixteen years, he began by being suddenly taken faint, like a man brought up with a short rope. That is more fishy still."

"I will have no buying off, or compromises," said Jack. "I will have the whole thing cleared up or not embarked in at all."

"So you shall," said the lawyer. "All the suitors say that at the beginning. It is an understood thing. Perhaps, as we get on, we shall see the necessity of a compromise. Now leave me to think things over. A partnership:

accounts never cleared up: a piece of land which was Armstrong's when he died, and was Bayliss's after he died: a great wind-bag of pretension and pride to burst. It may hurt us, but as I have nothing to lose, I don't care. One thing, Jack Armstrong," he said earnestly. "If . . . if this case comes to anything, make me your lawyer. You know me. I am not dishonourable; I am not unskilful; but I want friends."

"Is that all?" said Jack. "Of course I will."

CHAPTER XX.

The next morning Jack sought counsel of his lawyer again.

"I have been thinking of your affair all night. Now I have remembered a circumstance which may, or may not, be of use to us. First of all, however Bayliss got possession of the estate, he has held possession, undisputed, for upwards of twenty years."

"Yes. I am nearly twenty-three."

"That constitutes a title, unless we can prove that he gained it fraudulently. Now, before I was articled, I was a clerk in the old Bank, and I remember, ten years ago, seeing in the strong room a bundle of papers marked 'Title Deeds of Paul Bayliss, Esquire.' We must see these title deeds."

"That is so long ago. Most likely they have been taken out."

"It is most likely, on the other hand, that they are there. People let such things stay in safe places."

"Do you know any one at the Bank?"

"Yes; I know them nearly all, from manager to porter. I will try what can be done."

He left him, and Jack went to seek advice of Mr. Fortescue.

The old clergyman heard the tale, and sighed wearily.

"It is the old story, I suppose," he said. "There will be a complication of interests. One man owes money to another; the other helps himself to payment, and defends his action. What can you prove? Your father and Mr. Bayliss were partners. Your father died; Mr. Bayliss went on."

"I will never give in," said Jack. "If I can prove that a single acre of my father's property ought to be mine, I will have it."

"Naboth's vineyard," said Mr. Fortescue. "No doubt the sons of Naboth were very disagreeable to Ahab's successors till they got back their own again. Well, Jack, you must have your own way. Tell your lawyer that I will call upon him."

"You are very good, sir. You are always more than good to me; but I will try to fight my own battles first."

"Fight him, Jack," said Myles. "Fight him. Make the pompous old rascal give it all back again—every farthing. It's yours. I know it. I remember your poor father, as well as if it was yesterday, telling all the world one night, and only a few nights before the fire, that there was still a bit of land left for the child that was coming. That was the bit of land; and to think that I found the iron on it that night when Cardiff—— I beg your pardon, Arthur——"

"Not at all, Mr. Cuolahan," answered the boy, who was half asleep by the fire. "Not at all. I hope I am not in your way."

"By no means," returned Myles. "In my way, bless you? The innocent!" he murmured. "Well, Jack, it was that very identical night I dug up the turf for that ould villain Bastable while you were——well, never mind where you were," with a glance at the boy.

"Where was Jack, Mr. Cuolahan?" asked Arthur, with an air of the greatest interest.

"This is one of his stories, Norah. I will get it all out of him presently."

Then he shook his venerable locks.

"Jack," said Norah, "do not be vindictive."

"I will not, Norah; but I will fight."

"We are all sinners," said Myles, "till Norah pulls us up. Norah, alaunah! you ought to have been a preacher and a boy. Faith, and a broth of a boy, and a broth of a preacher you'd have made!"

"But you will be sure, Jack, that you are right before you fight, will you not?"

"I am sure already," said Jack, with the confidence of a prophet. "I *know* it; though whether I can prove it is a different thing. But I know it. My father's sudden death left Bayliss free. No one asked any questions. He let me go under Myles's charge, and then, when I was out of the place, sat down quietly and took possession of the land, little thinking what it was worth. The vein cropped up within a few inches of the turf, too, and might have been discovered by any one."

"I discovered it," said Myles, with great pride. "If a vein was a bit of hard rock that smashed the spade and made my arms tingle for a week, then I discovered it, close by where that Bastable picked up a bit that was bruk, and looked at it hard, and then looked sideways at me, and then hurried off by himself. He went to sell his secret, I'm thinking."

"Did he know who was the owner of the field?"

"How could he? He hadn't been in the place for more than a year or two, when he married that Keziah woman, his wife. To think that she was an Esbrough girl, born and bred, and me not to know it when I took you there to do the hanky-panky, Jack. No, Bastable knew nothing. And what will you do next, Jack?"

The lawyer easily ascertained that the deeds were still in the Bank, and he then went before one of the magistrates and made an affidavit, by virtue of which he obtained an injunction to restrain the delivery of the deeds to Mr. Bayliss, and liberty to take copies of them.

And the same day he wrote to Paul Bayliss, calling upon him, in the name of Jack

Armstrong, to produce the accounts of his partnership with John Armstrong, deceased.

Bayliss was sitting at breakfast, Ella pouring out his tea.

"I used to think, Ella," he said, "that young Armstrong was better than most young fellows. But he is worse, Ella; he is worse."

She looked at him with surprise.

"They are all alike. Everybody looks after himself in this world. Where is gratitude? Where is common honesty? Young Smith, to whom I gave eighty pounds a year, forges a cheque and bolts. Young Armstrong——"

"Jack Armstrong?" The girl turned pale and red, but her father did not notice her. He was spreading butter in thick slabs on his toast.

"Young Armstrong," he went on, "who is really a clever lad, goes to Germany, picks up some knowledge, and comes back with it, offering to sell it to me—to ME, the man who took him in as an apprentice for nothing—and what do you think he wants for it?"

"I am sure I cannot tell."

"Nothing but a partnership, Ella," he replied, with his grandest air. "Nothing but a partnership. Think of that! This young upstart."

"Oh! papa. And you've often told me that the Armstrongs were once the owners of all Esbrough."

"What does that matter? He hasn't got a penny. He's a beggar. He lives on the charity of old Fortescue. And he actually has the audacity to propose to be my partner. Yes, John, give me the letters."

Ella got her letters and began to read them. When she had finished she looked up.

Her father was sitting opposite her, rigid, his eyes fixed; the blood had left his face, which was pale and sunken; his trembling hands held the letter which he had just read. His lips were shaking as if he was trying to articulate words.

"Father!"

He neither moved nor spoke.

Then she started up and took his hand.

The letters rustled.

"No," he said, in a hoarse voice. "No. Don't dare touch them. Don't dare read them. Go away, girl. Be off, I say."

Paul Bayliss had once or twice in his life been rough with his daughter, but never like this.

"How dare you touch my letters? How dare you offer to read what is sent to me?"

"Papa," she cried, "I never thought of touching them. I never dreamed of reading them."

He stood up and stared about the room with a wild look of terror.

Then he turned to his daughter, the pretty child whom he had brought up so tenderly, and who winced beneath his eyes like a frightened pet.

"Forgive me, Ella," he said. "A sudden attack—what was it? A giddiness. I am better now—better now—much better now."

"Will you have the doctor, papa?"

"No, I want no doctor," he groaned. What bodily disease? what pain and suffering would not have been preferable to this blow? "I want no doctor—now!"

"Will you take something, papa?"

"Give me a glass of brandy. There, don't ring. Go and get it."

He sank back again, while his daughter

went for the spirits, and tried to understand the position.

She brought the decanter with a liqueur glass. He drank three, one after the other.

"Ella," he whispered, "do not breathe a word of this attack. It is the second I have had in my life. The first was when—when—when young Armstrong was brought to me by Cuolahan, seven or eight years ago. I thought I had got over that. And now he comes back again, and I have another. The boy will be the death of me. Don't say a word, Ella, mind. If you chatter I will never forgive you. Do you hear? I will cut you off with a shilling. . . . My poor Ella." He took her terror-stricken face in his hands and kissed it. "My poor Ella, we do not know what a day may bring forth. Yesterday I was strong and proud; to-day I am weak and humble—and afraid," he added, "afraid."

"You are ill, papa. You are not yourself. Let me send for the doctor."

"No. I am going to the study.. Leave me there. If I want anything I will ring, and you shall answer the bell. Leave me by myself."

He took his letters and went to his own room, a room fitted up with shelves, full of books which he never read, desks and writing-tables which he never used, and paper on which he never wrote. Then he locked the door and sat down, and buried his head in his hands to think.

The first thing he did, curiously, was to go fast asleep. No opiate could have laid him more completely at rest than the sudden blow he had just received.

It was nine o'clock. At twelve he awoke with a start of surprise, with an uneasy and anxious look, with a sudden pang at the heart that brought him back to his misery. Count up, reader, if you can, the few nights in your life when you have had dreams of a rapture so great and glorious as to lift you up to heaven. You will find that they were the nights preceding your most unhappy days, when you had sought your bed with the misery of impending suffering, anxious to bury yourself in forgetfulness for but a few hours. You awake, and the transition is so dreadful as to magnify your present woe tenfold. So Bayliss,' waking from a dream of some great bliss, in which he, Paul, was clothed with white raiment and crowned with gold, and led forth before his fellows as the Great, the Good, the Only One, suddenly remembered the letters that lay on the table, and straightway his heart fell like lead.

"I am a fool," he said, "I am a fool. Every man can be bought off. The boy wants money."

Then he read the letters again.

"The Bank stops the deeds. Oh! that I had taken them out two days ago, as I intended. Let me answer this."

He took his pen and wrote. His hand was shaky, and the words would not form themselves. He made half a dozen copies, and at last was satisfied.

"Dear Stewart," he said. Observe that his style was generally "Dear sir," or "Sir," *tout court*. "Dear Stewart, I have received your mysterious communication: keep the deeds by all means. When you can find time to let me know the nature of the threat implied, do so. I may tell you *in confidence*, that I have had another letter inviting me to render an account of my partnership with the late John

Armstrong. That was dissolved twenty-two years ago. Please tell me if you have those books among the rest of my papers. And if so, keep them as well as the deeds. I am too busy to look into these petty things myself, but you can tell me if you want help, and I will get my London solicitor to advise."

He read this over a dozen times. Yes, it was bold; it was fearless; it treated the affair as beneath contempt. And then he read the other letter.

"Produce the accounts!" he ground his teeth. "I think I see myself producing the accounts. Why, I burned them twenty years ago. All but the memorandum-book."

He opened a drawer and took out a little book.

"Everybody may read this," he said. "F. G. to A. B. That means Johnny Armstrong to Paul Bayliss. Five hundred pounds—two hundred pounds—one hundred pounds. Paul Bayliss, face the thing. Tell yourself the beastly truth. Truth is always beastly. You never had a penny. You took loan upon loan from Johnny Armstrong and his wife, though it went in drink. You had the luck of the devil, and you lost it as fast as you got it. Then came the fire, and the father died, and the child was carried away. No one knew about the loans, for the papers were all in my hands, and I burned them all. So far I am safe—safe. I can say that the books were with the senior partner and were burned with the fire. Who is to say they were not? And then the land—the field—the only point that I have got to face. I have held it for twenty-three years. But I for—I wrote the deed, and signed it. Witnessed by Jacob Kislingbury, clerk to the parish. Dead!— good man. And by Benjamin Bastable, lawyer's clerk. Where is he? Can he ever come back? No. He would have come to me for money. And yet. . . . "

He looked at his watch. It was only one o'clock. He got up, and looked at his face in the glass. It was transformed. The confident bearing had gone out of it. The pride had gone. A look of cunning, fear, and treachery was in their place. And one who knew Paul Bayliss well might have said that the look had been there always, hidden under a thin varnish of simulated self-respect.

One o'clock. He burned to know if Bastable had returned. But how to find out? He could not prowl about the streets, searching for Bastable.

He ordered his carriage. Ella came furtively from her hiding-place to know if he was better. He greeted her kindly.

"I am not well, dear; but I am better. I am going to the office on business, and shall be home early. Don't fuss about me, Ella."

At the works he sent for Hodder.

"Do you remember, Hodder, a man who was about the place some years ago? Let me see. When first we hit on the vein, and before I took up the Ravendale mines—a man named Bastable?"

"I remember him well, sir. He used to talk about mesmerism and spirits."

"The same. He went away, I believe."

"Yes, sir; went to America. And never came back."

"Oh! never came back. I have a reason for wishing to see that man, Hodder. You are sure he never came back?"

"Quite sure, sir. If he had come back, his wife would have told me."

"His wife?"

"Yes, sir. He married my second cousin, Keziah Kislingbury, and deserted her. She's living with a lady in the Ravendale Road, Mrs. Merrion, a widow companion I think she calls herself."

It was lucky that Bayliss's back was turned to the speaker, or his look of terror and agony would have been noticed. A moment or two passed in silence. Then Bayliss spoke in a harsh and unnatural voice.

"Send me a boy, Hodder, to fetch Mrs. Bastable; or, no, I cannot write. Go yourself and bring her. With Mrs. Merrion! Living with Adelaide!—and I never knew."

Then, as one in some trouble, he sat down by the fire and waited. They brought him cheques to sign—he signed them all without a word. They brought him orders for approval—he approved them all; they brought him reports, which he laid upon the table. And with the swiftness of a telegraphic message, the news ran through the works that employed a thousand men, girls, and boys, that their revered and dreaded chief was ill.

Ill he was in mind, and sore cast down.

But Paul Bayliss was not going to throw up the sponge.

"I will buy them 'off," he said, "I will buy them off. Young Armstrong, curse him, shall have everything—promised; and as soon as I get the deeds I will burn them, and laugh in all their faces—damn them!"

Then came Hodder with Mrs. Bastable.

"Are you Mrs. Bastable?"

"I am, sir," said Keziah, quietly.

"What do you know about this business?" uttered Bayliss abruptly. "No," he went on, "How should you? Where is your husband, Mrs. Bastable?"

"I wish I knew, sir."

"Then he has not come back?"

"No, sir; he has not come back."

"Swear it—swear upon the Bible. No; why should you tell me lies? So he has not come back—not come back—and no one knows where he is? So, so. That is good."

He was talking half aloud in his excitement. "Mrs. Bastable, you will tell me when he does come back, will you not, *if* he does come back?"

"Lord, sir! Yes, I will tell you; not that

it makes any difference to you where that wife-deserter has gone to."

"Well, only promise to tell me—then—then. And so, Mrs. Bastable, you live with Mrs. Merrion? and how is it I have never seen you there?"

"You have, sir, plenty of times, only you did not notice me."

"Ah! perhaps not. And how is my lovely widow, eh, Mrs. Bastable, eh? How is the charming Adelaide? Give her my compliments, will you, and say that I hope to run up and call upon her to-night."

The danger in his mind once removed, Bayliss became sportive again.

Bastable not back? Why, that would give him time. He would buy them off.

He took no notice of the letter ordering him to produce his accounts, went home, had a pleasant little dinner in his own study, making his illness of the morning a reason for dining alone and early, drank a bottle of port, and then drove back to his office. There he left his carriage and walked to Mrs. Merrion's, where he spent a charming evening with the widow.

CHAPTER XXI.

In the land of repentance it is always morning, and the sinners feel their position upon water only, no intoxicating drinks or other incentives to re-enter the paradise of fools being allowed. Mr. Bayliss awoke rather earlier than usual to the recollection that he was in a perilous state, and his spirits fell in one moment to the lowest point of despondency.

"Bastable is dead," he kept on saying to himself. "Bastable is dead long ago. Who can say anything? Who can find out? At the worst, I will buy them off. . . . After all these years. . . . If I could get hold of those papers!"

He breakfasted in his study, telling Ella that he was better, but had a headache; and then, because he was restless, sent away his carriage, and walked into town.

He fancied the people looked at him as he walked along the road. They did; not because he had forged a deed, and was afraid of being found out, but because he swung heavily along the road, his coat-tails flying behind him, in a quick, nervous way, different to his usual pompous walk. Then his face looked queer. The great red cheeks were pale; nervous twitching pulled his lips one way and the other; and his eyes were fixed.

He went straight to the Bank, arriving there a moment after the doors were opened.

"What is this business, Stewart, that you wrote to me about? I was too much engaged yesterday to look into it."

The manager shut the door.

"Those deeds of yours on which we advanced you money twelve years ago."

"Well; and what about those deeds?"

"They have filed an affidavit which—which—in fact, orders us to stop the deeds; and they have taken copies."

The manager noticed that his client changed colour, and he suspected *why*. He was an Esbrough man, and he knew the history of Johnny Armstrong. He suspected now why Paul Bayliss trembled and shook before him.

"You are not well, Mr. Bayliss; sit down."

"No; I am not well. I was ill all day yesterday, and I am worse to-day. . . They have taken copies, you said?"

He sat down, and tried to pull himself together.

"Yes, they took them yesterday; that is to say, young Clifton, who is acting for Armstrong, took them. You had better see your lawyer, Mr. Bayliss. A thing of this kind may be only a threat to extort money, though young Mr. Armstrong is not the man likely to do that."

"I am half mad, I think. What shall I do, Stewart? You know all about money matters. They want me to show my accounts of partnership with Armstrong's father. How can I? The books were burned in the fire that killed him."

"Your offices were not burned."

"No; but my partner had taken the books home with him to examine. It was not usual for him to do that; but as we'd had a dispute, things were going badly with us both, he had the books with him—had taken them, in fact, the very afternoon, after office hours, when the fire occurred."

"Well, that is one thing. But why do they want to copy the title-deeds?"

"I do not know. How should I know?"

"Well, Mr. Bayliss, no one knows of this business except ourselves, and as it is always delicate and dangerous work, raking up old affairs, I should think you might compromise; a few hundreds or so are nothing to you. This young man is the son of his father; he naturally wants to know what became of the family property. Take him into confidence, and make a friend of him."

There was a look in the banker's eyes which the millionaire did not like. Paul shook hands with him like some poor suppliant begging for help, and then he crept away, the clerks staring with wonder at his crestfallen look.

The manager, when he was gone, sent for the hall porter, an old man who had been a servant of the Bank for fifty years.

He gave the man a few commissions, and began to talk carelessly to him.

"Did you see Mr. Bayliss this morning?"

"I did, sir, and very ill he looked. When I gave him the good-morning, he never answered."

"Yes, he seems ill. But he's getting on in age. How old is he?"

"Paul Bayliss? Let me see. I am sixty-seven. Paul Bayliss must be a good ten years younger. Fifty-seven, he is, I should say. Same age as poor Johnny Armstrong."

"You remember the death of his partner, I suppose?"

"Lord, sir, as if it was yesterday! It was New Year time, and we'd had a busy time here with people all day long paying in and drawing out. Johnny Armstrong came just before the shutters went up, and saw the manager. Poor fellow! It was four o'clock; and if he'd gone home to his wife, he might have been alive to this day."

"Did he not go home to his wife, then?"

"No; he went back to his office, and then he went to the public-house, and there he stayed till he went home drunk at ten o'clock, and set fire to his house and burned the place down, and himself too."

"Oh!" said Mr. Stewart. "You are sure he did not go home between four and ten?"

"Sure. Why, it was all in the inquest. Mr. Bayliss gave his evidence, and said so."

"Ah! did he? That will do."

The Bank manager lay back and whistled softly.

"I very much fear," he said, with an admixture in his expression of that joy which people feel at witnessing the woes of others, "I very much fear that we are going to have a pretty scandal. Paul Bayliss, founder of the English Chicago, as they say in the papers, the king of iron masters, the employer of thousands, he to whom thousands look for their daily bread, as well as for their guidance and example—Paul Bayliss has been doing something queer. Let us see these papers."

He got the papers which were stopped, and turned over the pages. Among them was a conveyance, as short and simple as such documents can be made. It gave Paul Bayliss Johnny Armstrong's last bit of land.

The witnesses were Samuel Kislingbury,

clerk to the parish church, and Benjamin Bastable, lawyer's clerk. It was dated a month before the death of Armstrong.

The manager took another opportunity of talking with the old porter.

"I suppose," he said, "you remember all the old Esbrough people?"

"Bless you, sir! yes, every one. Most of them here still, some up and some down."

"Mostly up, I suppose."

"I don't know, sir. There's myself and my boys, just like my old father and his boys. Where we are, there we stick. Some folk are like burrs, you know. Well, and some are like thistledown, blown about the world, and never knowing where to settle. Look at Benjamin Bastable, now."

"Ay! ay! That is a strange name. Who is Benjamin Bastable?"

"He was a lawyer's clerk for one thing. He married Keziah Kislingbury; and then he turned magician: came down here with his wife just twelve years ago; then he ran away and left her. Never heard of again, and his wife a lone woman to this day."

"Thistledown—yes, like thistledown. Bastable was a native of this place, I suppose?"

"Oh no! not an Esbrough chap at all. He came about two and twenty years ago, just after poor Johnny Armstrong died!"

He looked again at the deed. Bastable had only come to that town after the death of Armstrong. It was dated, as I have said, a month before the death.

"By the Lord! it's a forgery, and a clumsy one," he said to himself. "The Bank never examined it, and Bayliss, like a fool, never destroyed it."

Paul Bayliss resolved on a plan of action that evening, after a bottle and a half of port; his courage being thus screwed up to the point of taking the broadest ditches at a flying leap.

"I will send for the boy to-morrow," he said; "we will have no more to do with lawyers. I will take him into partnership. He shall have what he wants. He shall have more than he wants. By Gad! he shall be a full partner in the whole concern. And he shall marry Ella, if he likes. He cannot find out anything. I wrote it in an engrossing hand. I copied a deed word for word. I wrote the signatures so that the devil himself could not find out the difference. The clerk is dead, and Bastable gone away—dead too, likely. What have I to fear? It's a bugbear. Bastable dead? Of course he is dead. He went to America with the money I gave him. He told me that if he wanted any more he should write to me, and he hasn't written. Of course he is dead, long ago. And a good thing too."

Then he drank another glass of port, and began to walk up and down the room.

"Why should not Armstrong be my partner? He is the son of my former partner. And why shouldn't I let him marry Ella, if I like? It's a good match on both sides: we'll call it a love match, and young Perrymont may go after that Norah girl."

He went into the drawing-room, where Ella was sitting alone.

"Yes, dear. Don't ask me how I am, because it worries and does no good. I'm ill, but I dare say I shall be better soon. Give me a cup of tea, will you?"

He sat down and sighed wearily, looking round the great splendid room, in one corner of which his daughter sat like a fairy in a glade. All these glories threatened to depart from him, like a dream.

"I am getting old, Ella," he said, forgetting the tea. "I am getting old. Don't interrupt me, child. I have been thinking of taking a partner."

"Yes, papa."

"I sometimes think that young Armstrong would be the right man to succeed me. The son of my old friend and partner, you know. Who fitter? We were not always so rich as we are now, Ella, though you may not remember it."

"I remember it well, papa—the little house in—"

"There, there; we need not be so minute. We were poor and we are rich, that is enough. I will talk to Armstrong to-morrow. It is almost time, Ella, to find you a partner, too."

"Oh! papa. I am in no hurry."

"Right, Ella, right. The man I mean is—is—but I will not tell you his name. Go to bed, my dear, and dream of wedding-bells and orange-blossoms."

"And you, papa, will dream of getting better, will you not?"

"I will dream that I am well again. Ha! ha! there is nothing the matter with me, nothing at all. Only a little spasm now and then. Good-night, Ella, good-night."

The girl went away.

Presently her father went to bed too.

In the room of the girl, dainty with pretty hangings and costly trifles, a little head in a whirl with the thought of the strange thing that was going to happen to her. In the other, a massive apartment, where a huge four-poster with immense curtains stood in the centre of a room filled with massive mahogany furniture, Paul Bayliss lying asleep and dreaming heavily.

He has not extinguished the lights, which are turned down low enough to cast deep shadows across the room. The sleeping, gross red face is purple as he pushes it deeper into the pillow; the veins stand out in the dim light like black ropes upon his forehead; his hands are stretched out upon the bed and clutch the sheets. Paul Bayliss is far away from his splendid mansion. Curiously enough, he is, in spirit, sitting upright, looking about him. He knows that it is night, but somehow he sees clearly. He thinks he is in a small and narrow room, the walls of which are white-washed; above him is a little window, with bars across it; he is sitting on a mattress spread over a bench; there is a Bible at his elbow; he wonders where he is. Then he hears footsteps outside; a rap comes at his door.

"Number a hundred and twenty-eight."

"Here," he replies, mechanically, and then he remembers, suddenly, that he is in prison.

In prison; Paul Bayliss the millionaire in prison.

His position, the judge had remarked, only aggravated the offence. He had gone on for twelve years enjoying the proceeds of his crime. He had grown enormously rich through that crime; he had through that crime attained to an eminence that made his fall only the more signal, and ought to make his punishment the more exemplary. The boy who was the rightful owner of all that he possessed was working, a common apprentice with the rest, in his works. For him he had done nothing. Nay, more; when the boy returned from the continent.

and timidly offered to make him still richer at the price of a small share in the new formation of wealth, he had driven him away with words of contempt. The jury had not the power of bringing in another verdict. The evidence of the crime was complete. First, there was the absence of the legal technicalities, owing to the pretended deed being a slavish copy. Then there was the witness of the expert, who swore that the signatures were all written by the same hand; then the testimony of Keziah Bastable, who swore that her husband was not in Esbrough at the time of the signature; and lastly, the most damning circumstance of all, the water-mark in the paper was of more recent date. Truly, as the counsel for the prosecution observed, the prisoner was a clumsy forger. It was evident that this was his first crime. It was the act of an avenging Providence that he seemed to have actually forgotten the existence of the forgery, when he might any day have removed all evidence of the crime. The judge had gone on to point out to the public that a long course of selfish indulgence—it seemed an unusual line for a judge to take—had not only blinded the moral perception of the prisoner, but also probably partially destroyed his memory. At any moment he might have taken away the deeds and destroyed the forgery, when, no copy being in existence, he might have laughed at the law. Any day might bring his destruction. And as if it were not enough that all this array of witnesses should appear against him, at the last moment, during the trial, the man Bastable himself had appeared and sworn that he had never signed any such deed; had sworn, besides, that he had himself discovered the vein of iron on the property, and had taken three thousand pounds as a reward out of the first profits made, on the condition of going away. It was rare indeed, the judge said, that the annals of crime offered an instance so remarkable of infatuation. He should say little more to aggravate the misery and remorse of the prisoner, but would sentence him to ten years' penal servitude.

Fool that he had been! Fool at every point. With the game in his own hand, the cards all trumps, and but one wrong card, he had deliberately played it.

Ten years. Ten years to be locked up, silent and alone in a white-washed cell; ten years to have no society but the chaplain, no change but the Sunday chapel; no book but the Bible—it would drive him mad. He seemed to rise and prowl up and down the little room. No pleasure, no joy, no pride of life any more; and when he came out of his prison hiding in oblivion for the rest of his days.

"I shall be sixty-seven!" he answered. "I shall be sixty-seven, and an old man. Ella will hate me; not one of my friends will speak to me. It is bad now—but oh!—my God! it will be worse then. Ten years to wait! Perhaps a ticket-of-leave. And this only the second day!"

He awoke with a groan, the beads standing on his forehead—awoke and sat upright in his bed, and looked round with a wild stare.

He saw only the white walls of his cell; the familiar furniture of his own room was as a dream; he was asleep still, and beside him stood the ghost of his dead partner.

"Paul," said poor Johnny, "I was a bad man, and I wasted everything in drink. But you had my bit of land left, and there was the boy. You had all that borrowed money, too; could you not have paid it back to him, at least with some of the interest? It's too late now. We are both sinners, Paul, but you are the worst. I never deserted a friend; I never forged a deed; I never turned my back upon the poor; I paid my debts. Now you are in prison, Paul—in prison for ten long years. You will have to work all day; you will be alone all night; you will have no drink, and I shall come and sit with you, when there is no one to interrupt us, and I will talk to you, Paul Bayliss, for the sake of old times."

With a wild tossing of his arms, the wretched man awoke, and found it was but two o'clock, and that it was all a dream.

CHAPTER XXII.

The night passed slowly on. What a night would that be when the veil of self-deception was wholly withdrawn and the cruel naked truth left like some steep wall of granite cliff up which a man cannot climb, while the relentless tide sweeps slowly up the shore, to drown and destroy him. The wretched man paced his lonely room, tossing his arms in his unrest. He turned on the lights full; he lit the candles that stood upon the mantelshelf; he fancied that behind him stood the ghost of his partner, accusing, grim, hideously threatening; —and before him, around him, above him, was the cell with its narrow walls, the stone bench, the Bible, and the ten years' sentence ringing in his ears. It was a dream, a nightmare, if you like, but such a dread as had the horrid semblance of prophecy; such a nightmare as personated a reality. So might Ahab have tossed in his sleep after the murder of Naboth; so might David, in his cedar palace, have seen at his bedside the murdered form of the man whom Joab had put at his bidding in the foremost front of the battle.

From time to time he lay down, but not to sleep. For when his eyes closed there rose up again before him the grisly phantom of the prison, and he started again with an oath and a prayer alternate, to find relief in pacing up and down. Oh! slow and weary night to those who sleep not! Oh! swift and happy night to him who sleeps and wakes in the arms of one who loves him! Great and solemn mystery of night! when each withdraws from his fellows, and, perforce, communes with himself; when the paradise of imagination fades away, and that grim fortress of fact which is so like a prison shows clear and strong.

It was late in December, when the sun rises at seven. Paul Bayliss dressed himself at daybreak, and wandered forth in the stately gardens, wet now with continual dews, to seek rest and comfort. Rest and comfort there were none; the day dawned slowly—so slowly, with great banks of cloud; the cold trees, clothed with a scanty vestment of yellow leaves, stood round him, and seemed to point their branches, threatening and pitiless, at his face; the air was heavy and silent. The great house before him, which he had built himself, seemed staring at him behind the white blinds of the windows in a sad surprise; and Paul Bayliss, for the first time in his life, sank upon a bank and dropped his head in his hands and shed tears that rolled pitifully down his cheeks. It is not only the innocent hunted hare that weeps; the fox himself, after ten thousand shifts and turns have been tried, and all to no avail, will weep when the inevitable end is close to him.

"It is hard," he murmured, "after what I have achieved—after this great and splendid career, to lose all for a single act of folly—of crime—call it crime, what does it matter? It is done; it must be faced. Fool! to be terrified at a nightmare, at an undigested dinner, at a shadow, at less than a shadow, at nothing at all!"

He tried to reason with himself, but it was of little avail, for in his heart he *knew* the future that might be, and the days of bitterness which nothing but a miracle could avert. We are all of us so; we have a Cassandra-like power of prophecy, inasmuch as, like the prophets to the kings of Israel, we, if we foretell anything concerning ourselves, foretell only disaster. And it always comes true. Paul Bayliss knew that he was found out. It was maddening to think that in their quiet beds lay sleeping young Jack Armstrong and Clifton the lawyer, the arbiters of his fate, while he was here cold, comfortless, and wretched, the King of Esbrough, waiting for what might please these dependents of his to do to him.

He walked through the wicket gate at the back of his garden, and plunged into the plantation behind—his own plantation, his own planting. The ground was knee deep with the wet and fragrant fallen leaves; on the branches sat the pretty pheasants, too lazy to move, although the light was strong; the scarlet berries hung upon the mountain-ash, the holly was bright with red, a few wildflowers lingered still where the cold winds could not touch them, and the rays of the sun could warm them yet. He trampled on them regardless. Presently he came to a pool; he knew it well because he had caused it to be made; it was deep, so as to drain the coppice; it was broad, so broad that, as he thought, a man might lie at the bottom with no chance of being fished out; it was black to look at, and covered with a thick film of weed that might serve, he thought, as a fitting pall for one whose life had ended in sudden and terrible collapse. Should he end it so? As he stood and played with the thought, a thousand memories flashed across him, and all his life lived over again. It is so at decisive moments of our fate; we stand upon the brink and remember, not what will be, but what has been; the girl who answers the letter of her lover and remembers all the sweetness of the household she is going to give up: the youth who pauses before he commits the fatal act that robs him of his honour: the man who changes his fate by the stroke of a pen, they pause to think of the past. Paul Bayliss stood upon the brink. Why not end it? They call it cowardice, this temptation to end it all, when life becomes too dreadful to bear. Is it altogether cowardice? I think not. The future we know not; the present we know; whatever the future can give, we think it will be better than the dreadful present. Alas! we cannot tell that the present will always live with us. Like the exile who runs across the sea, we may change the sky, but not the wind. Paul Bayliss stood hesitating on the brink. One plunge, and it was done; one cold plunge into the weed-covered pool; one bubble rising to the surface, and his despair would be finished for ever. For ever! Who can tell? and if we were certain that such an act would cut the knot and set the captive free, be sure that not a living man but would be tempted at some moments of his life to take the knife and sever the silver thread. One plunge! he looked and thought. Above him the clouds parted and the fog lifted and the sun rose broad and glorious, though it was but a morning in December. The birds began to sing round him—not the summer birds which come for a season and leave us all through the time when most we want the beauty of their softness and their song, but those sad-coloured birds which belong to all the year. But he sees nothing, he hears nothing; his eyes are fixed upon the black, cold water; he is thinking of the terrible future that may await him, and he is summoning his courage for the leap. He will take it—he will be free; farewell to the miseries of despair and ruin—farewell to nights of terror and days of suspense; he will bear no more.

He raises his arms as in the attitude of one who will spring from the bank.

A step, a whistle, a voice! It is his own gamekeeper, gun on shoulder, dog at heel, who tramples through the underwood, cracking the dead twigs, breaking off the dead branches, tearing through the trailing arms of the blackberry bushes. Paul Bayliss recovers himself suddenly, and looks round him. It is a bright and glorious morning, the red sun shines in his face and brings back its colour; he turns his head, and lo! the phantoms of the nightmare disappeared, and Paul Bayliss is strong again.

His keeper was surprised to see him.

"Good day, sir. Out very early this morning, sir."

"Yes; I could not sleep. I got up to try the fresh air."

"Very good thing for you, sir. Beg pardon, sir. Try it every morning, sir."

"Ay! ay! well . . . yes . . . we will have a day here soon—as soon as you like. . ."

The master turned and walked back to the house a different man. His step was elastic, his heart was light; his thoughts were high again. What had worked the miracle? Sunshine and light.

Paul Bayliss, who had been repentant, softhearted, sorry, pricked up his ears and looked about him. He was himself again, a foxterrier, not thoroughbred, because he had a touch of the mastiff. He felt, through all his veins, the old familiar instincts of courage. His troubles, however, were not over.

He sat in his study at breakfast alone.

The footman came in, deferential and quiet.

"A person, sir, wants to see you."

"A gentleman?"

"No, sir, not exactly a gentlemen. Rather looks like a common man, sir. Couldn't get his name. Said it was no consequence, sir; and if you didn't see him, he could go down to the works."

"Well, let him come in. And, John, see that he wipes his boots."

The person came in: a short, fat man, with a large fringe of reddish-grey beard, short, and thick-set—a man who, unlike most men, conveyed no idea of any profession whatever. You can generally make a good guess at a man's habitual work, especially if you have visited the favourite publics of the trades at meal hours. But this man might have been anything. There was a shifty look about his eyes; his mouth was full, and his lips prominent; he was strongly built; his hands were white, and his fingers long and delicate—such fingers as belong to men skilled in musical instruments. And he was dressed, apparently, to look as much like an undertaker as could be managed out of a second-hand suit of rusty black.

He came in, deposited his hat on the floor, and sat down. Then he turned slowly to Paul Bayliss.

"You do not remember me, Mr. Bayliss?"

Mr. Bayliss did remember him. He flushed for a moment, and held his breath. Then, while great beads stood upon his swollen forehead, he went to his writing-desk.

"Excuse me one moment, sir," he said.

"I have a note to write, and I will be at your service."

He wrote his note.

"My dear Armstrong,

"Come and see me instantly—instantly. I am ill, and I have a good deal to see to. Do not take any steps whatever, and let none be taken. I have to talk to you of your father.

"Your father's oldest friend,

"Paul Bayliss."

Then he rang the bell, moving with uncertain step and a quick, anxious manner. The footman came, and he despatched the note with a whisper.

"Take it yourself, James. If Mr. Armstrong is not at the cottage, look for him at Mr. Clifton's, the lawyer. Give it into his own hand, and bring me the answer. Be quick, and be sure."

The man took the epistle, and retired.

Then Mr. Bayliss turned to his visitor.

"Now, Mr.—— I don't know your name, sir."

"And yet it is only a dozen years since we met, Mr. Bayliss; only a dozen years when Esbrough was only a little market town. Surely you remember me!"

"Let me think. I see so many faces."

"But not many like mine, Mr. Bayliss."

That was true. It was so seamed and wrinkled; there were such multitudinous crow's feet about the eyes; such lines crossing and intercrossing about the forehead; such furrows about the mouth, that it was quite reasonable to suppose his face to be one of the rarest extant.

"Think again, Mr. Bayliss."

"Upon my word, I believe you are Mr. Bastable."

"And your belief is like the Apostles' Creed, Mr. Bayliss, because it's every word true."

"Mr. Bastable, Mr. Bastable, I thought when we parted that you had received so large a compensation for your discovery, of which I confess that I have profited, that you agreed not to return to this place."

"I did, Mr. Bayliss."

"I have even your promise in writing not to return, not to ask for anything more—to be content, in fact."

"You have, Mr. Bayliss, there's no denying it."

"Then what do you want of me?"

The man shifted his legs, and appeared uneasy.

"What have you been doing since you were here last? You began by deserting your wife, who is, I am told, now living in this town?"

"Well, I left her, that is true; I had enough of her. So would you, Mr. Bayliss, if you'd married Keziah Kislingbury. There, I defy any man, if he got the chance, not to desert Keziah, though she had her gifts—and wonderful they were. Perhaps I was a fool not to stick to them. But there, you see where the land lay. I thought, with my knowledge of metals, that I'd nothing to do but just to go to America and dig the gold in pailfuls. Now, no luck came of that three thousand pounds. Not a single cent did I net by it. It was payin' out and payin' out, like the sailors in a deep anchorage, and no bottom after all. I went to Colorado, where the silver mines are; no good. Then I went to Mexico prospecting; no good again. Then I tried Chili; no good there. And then I tried Australia. It took time; but the money was going faster and faster. Then I tried the diamond fields. Well, then, Mr. Bayliss, I suppose you'll believe *me* "—he spoke as if he was an Evangelist at least—" when I tell you that the diamond fields is the cussedest plant out. There is certainly them as find the stones, but there's them as finds none. I was one of them as found none—not a stone, not a single precious stone, not a damned diamond did I hit upon. And all the money was gone—quite gone."

"And then?" Mr. Bayliss looked at his watch as a sign to his guest.

"And then? Ah! then I had a pretty free time for a bit among the Boers, as they call them. You see, the land is a dry land, and as there are no rivers to speak of, they get along with wells. Covered all over it is with a scrub; the farms dotted all about: here and there a house with a cattle kraal. What they want mostly is water. I took up the old trade, and went about with my divining rod. There were others in the same lay—there always is. Blest if I think an honest speculator can hit on the cleverest dodge, but somebody else is on it before him, and then envy and hatred and backbiting. Not one single lay is there in the whole wide world that an honest man can take up all by himself, and have a clear field and no favour."

Mr. Bastable should have chosen literature. There, at least, he would have found an atmosphere where no man envies another of the same craft, where all alike unite in speaking well of their brothers, and where honest effort ever meets with honest appreciation.

"A dozen of us, at least, up and down Orange River. None of them a patch on me: that was allowed. If any one did know where to lay his hand upon a well with the Patent Infallible Wonder-working Hazel Divining Wand, it was Benjamin Bastable. I made the fortune of a dozen of the crawling, lazy Dutchmen, who smoke all day long, and forget their benefactors; and no thanks—not a bit. Lord! when I think of the things I have done for that colony, my mouth feels like a bit of blotting-paper."

"You will take something, Mr. Bastable?"

"Thank you, Mr. Bayliss. You always were a gentleman, though we had words about the Ravendale business. However, to give good drink a name, I'll say bitter beer for choice. It's scarce in the colonies, and an Englishman little thinks of the blessings he's got till he misses the blessings he's lost. A quart, if you don't mind, Mr. Bayliss."

The beer came, and Mr. Bastable, taking the jug in his hands, drained its contents at a single draught.

" Good Lord! it's heavenly! I came home in a temperance ship : worked my passage— me that had gone out a saloon passenger and drank champagne with tip top New York society. Why, I was nearly marr—— Lord! I forgot."

" Go on, Mr. Bastable."

" I got home a week or so ago. Found my way here to look for you, and fell in with my wife. There's more misfortunes, sir. There's a double-extra distilled misfortune for you. They never come single. ' Bad luck,' as the hymn says ; ' Bad luck is like the fleas in June. I never did them harm. They cannot come by ones or twos, but always comes in swarms.' "

" Go on, Mr. Bastable."

Mr. Bayliss's face was set, expectant of something; he knew what, but did not dare show any anxiety.

"I met her, on my way here, yesterday afternoon; and it's all gone, Mr. Bayliss, it's all gone."

"What is all gone?"

"The power, sir, the beautiful power. It's all gone. She isn't afraid of me. I saw her across the road, and I came behind her for a bit, trying on the old dodges. That didn't fetch her. Then I walked up to her and took her by the arm. She started a bit. 'Benjamin!' she says. 'Benjamin it is,' I replied in a deep and solemn voice, such as I used to use. Then, if you'll believe *me*, sir, she began to laugh. 'What's this, Keziah?' I asked. 'It's so funny,' she says. 'Funny?' I asks, 'Funny,' she says. 'Why is it funny?' I asks. 'I heard you behind,' she says, 'and I never thought about you a bit, and yet I knew, somehow, the step; and it's actually my Benjamin come back.' Then I ordered her to come with me and do my bidding. Devil a bit would she stir. 'It's all gone, Benjamin,' she said. 'The sperruts has left me for years and years. Even old Peter went at last: and he was like a burr for stickiness. As for Katey, she went off with somebody else, and I don't think Katey was a bit better than she ought to be. Not a sperrut left; not a rap in the house; not a voice in the night; no fingers about my throat; no footsteps on the stairs; no trances, and no clairvoyonging—and praise the Lord for all His mercies! For I'm never going to be a witch no more.' 'Keziah Bastable,' I said, 'you'll come to your lawful lord and master, and obey him as you promised in your wedding vows.' 'Drat the wedding vows,' she said, like a heathen. Why, the very Caffre women respect their wedding vows, or else their husbands let 'em have it with a stick; and very proper too. 'Drat 'em,' said Keziah. 'Keziah,' I said, 'are you mad?' 'Not at all,' she replied. 'I'm in my right senses. You deserted me for twelve long years, and left me all alone with the ghosts. Now, *do* you think, Benjamin Bastable, now I've a'most forgotten it all, and it's all forgiven up above, that I'm going to take up again with all the wicked courses? No; I'm not afraid of you—not a bit. I defy you. Do your worst. I won't come back to you. I won't go clairvoyonging for you. I won't help you to call up the sperruts, to go answering your foolish questions, when they ought to be saying their prayers and singing their hymns, and so keep out of trouble, poor things. I won't do it, Benjamin, and so I tell you;' and just then there came along the street—— Mr. Bayliss, may I ask for another suck at that beer? Talking always makes me dry, and just now my throat—you'll believe *me*— is like a sponge in summer weather. Thank you, Mr. Bayliss. Thank you, James. Don't pour it out, because the jug's a good jug for drinking out of. The best jugs I know are what the gins in Australia—the niggers' wives, you know—carry."

"Go on, Mr. Bastable."

"Ay, ay, give me time. Now I'll go on, Mr. Bayliss."

The man hitched his chair closer and laid his face sideways, almost on a level with the table, so looking into the eyes of his entertainer, who never moved, but sat looking into space with white lips, and a face that had no expression whatever in it.

"Listen, Mr. Bayliss; this concerns you. I've slept on it, and I thought I should do better to come straight to you this morning with it. Listen, now."

"I am listening."

"It was young Armstrong that came along the street with another gentleman, the boy who was my page when I was in the clairvoyancy line; the boy who was with Myles Cuolahan when the divining rod found the iron; the boy whose father owned all the land."

"Go on, Bastable."

"The other gentleman, when Keziah had told her story, took me by the arm, friendly like. 'Come with me,' he says, 'come with me, Mr. Bastable, and let us have a talk.' I went with him. We had a drain, or I did, because young Mr. Armstrong seems but a poor hand at the drink, and then we went to Mr. Clifton's office. He began to ask a lot of questions which did not seem to me to have much to do with my wife—when I came here, how long I stayed here, what I did here, and so on till I cut up rough. Then, said Jack —I mean young Armstrong, 'Show it him.' So they pulled out a paper and showed me my name at the bottom of it. 'Is that your signature?' asked the lawyer."

He paused and took some more beer.

"Go on, Mr. Bastable."

"I made no answer. Mr. Bayliss, I have been a lawyer's clerk. I know a conveyance, sharp enough when I see one. You know whether that conveyance that they had copied *ever came out of a lawyer's office or not. You know whether that is my signature or not.*"

"You did not reply?"

"I did not. I said, 'Gentlemen, here's a plant upon innocence. I shouldn't have thought it of you, Mr. Armstrong — I shouldn't indeed. You want to trap me. You will find it hard to trap me. Perhaps you'll give me time to answer that question, gentlemen. I've dodged the parairy dog on his native heath, and tackled the python in the Mexican jungle. I've likewise cheated the Chinaman and done the Caffre, but I never answered a question in a hurry yet that I did not repent at leisure, so I'll take a day or two, perhaps three, to think it over quietly and argue the matter out as between gentlemen.' So I had one more drain and came away."

"Go on, Mr. Bastable." His voice was husky now, and his eyes were dim with watching; for the worst blow of all was fallen, and his fate seemed to hang upon the weight of a feather.

"Now, Mr. Bayliss, let us be friendly, you and me. I'm as tight as wax if I'm paid. Let that be the groundwork of all. I'm the boy to hold my tongue, go away, keep dark, slip over to America, do anything, if I'm paid. How much?"

Mr. Bayliss was silent.

"I am not an expensive man. I want an annuity. It is nothing to you, a hundred or two out of your big income. Give me three hundred, say. Make arrangements to let me have it quarterly, and I'm the most silent dog in the world."

"How can I trust you?" asked Bayliss.

"Trust me? You can trust me because I am on the point of starvation. If you do not give me a pound or two I shall have to go and beg of Keziah."

Bayliss put his hand into his pocket and pulled out a handful of gold and silver.

"Take that to live with. Can you be silent another day?" he whispered eagerly.

"Of course I can."

"See, Bastable. You have all to gain—all to gain—by silence. I admit nothing. I say nothing. Only be silent for a single day, and you shall have your reward."

"Mr. Bayliss, I will. I give you my sacred word of honour, if you'll believe ME, that I will say nothing."

"Come, then, to-morrow at eight—no, at nine—and you shall see me again. Go quietly to some hotel, or—better still, go out of the town—and—and—for God's sake don't get drunk."

"Benjamin Bastable," said the hero, "never did get drunk but once in all his life. That was at Ballarat when the miners were having an evening with swell's drink. They messed up curaçoa and gin and champagne and port and brandy. Lord! how drunk we were. Don't be afraid, Mr. Bayliss; there's no such thing as curaçoa and champagne in this miserable country, I believe. To-morrow at nine. And look here, sir," he clapped him on the back. To a man of fine susceptibilities it would have been an additional pang; to Paul Bayliss it brought comfort. "If that deed is the only thing, don't you be afraid. It's only me, and I'm like an owl for quietness."

He went away.

Then Paul Bayliss wearily rose, walked feebly up and down, and then—went to bed, and fell sound asleep.

CHAPTER XXIII.

Poor old Cardiff Jack was growing steadily weaker. He spent most of the day upon the sofa or in an easy chair wheeled to the fire. The boat he had rigged with so much care, the kite he had constructed, lay in his room unheeded. Sometimes he would read, sometimes he would sit and think, sometimes he would talk with Norah, but always with the perfect sweetness of manner that distinguished this remarkably well-bred boy.

His affection for Norah exceeded all bounds. His eyes followed her about the room and rested upon her while she sat at work. She gave him advice about everything; to her he opened out his heart.

"Norah," he said one morning after a long nap by the fire, waking suddenly into liveliness, "when I think of what I am going to be, all my life, it seems as if there were some ugly dream in my head, which prevents my thinking at all."

"Never mind the dream, Arthur. And do not think too much about the future."

"But I must, you know. What is a boy to think of but the future? You don't really believe, dear Norah, that I am going on all my life making boats and all that nonsense, do you?"

"Surely not, Arthur."

"I am going to Eton, where I shall study hard and become a great scholar; then I am going. . . . I do not know yet; my cousin Lucy—where is cousin Lucy? I thought I saw her just now, when I was asleep."

He closed his eyes again, as he always did, when something jarred between his real and imaginary life. When he awoke again, it was in a more despondent mood. He was thinking of his weakness and his ailments.

"What is it, Norah?" he murmured. "If I run about like other boys, I get tired at once. I can't jump as I used to do. I am always having to sit down. And then I've got a pain whenever I move my left arm, which won't go away. What does it mean?"

Norah hesitated.

"Do not be afraid, Norah," said the boy. "If it is anything unpleasant to tell me, let me know it all the same. You know I shall be a man some day, and must be brave."

"There are some boys, Arthur, who never become men."

"Do you mean, Norah, that they are foolish boys all their lives?"

"No, Arthur. I mean—— My poor boy, are you quite brave?"

"I see, Norah," he said, shaking his white locks, while a tear started to his eye. "You mean that there are some boys who . . . die."

Norah was silent.

"Die," he went on, "leave all the bright world and—and—cousin Lucy. . . . Why does not my cousin come to me? I have not seen her all day. Die—and be put in a black coffin, and be carried to the family vault in a hearse. Norah, you don't think, really and truly think, that I am going to die?"

"Death, Arthur, has nothing to do with funerals. If you die, think of what is before you. You will change this world for a better.

Ah! Arthur, you think that everything is bright and happy. My poor boy, you will escape the temptation of life; you will avoid the sin and wretchedness of the world. It is better so, much better so."

"And Lucy?"

"Hush! my dear. You have forgotten. You have had a long illness, and will never be quite well again. Try to remember that Lucy has gone before, and that you will see her again in this new world where you are going. Would you know Lucy again?"

"Know cousin Lucy? Why, Norah, you must be silly to ask such a question. Know Lucy, indeed!"

"Tell me what she was like, dear Arthur."

He laughed outright, forgetting for the moment about his approaching death and the glorious world, the reward of innocence which lay beyond.

"Lucy is a year and a half younger than I am. Lucy is not really my cousin, but we always call her cousin; she has got brown eyes, your shaped eyes, Norah, and such a lot of brown curls, the same colour. Everybody says she is the prettiest girl in the world; and when we grow up, we are going to marry. That is all arranged."

"But, Arthur, you can never marry Lucy now. She is gone before, you remember."

"I forgot—I must have been ill. Where is she gone?"

"Gone into the silent land, Arthur. Gone to heaven, where you are going soon."

"You think I shall go there soon? Norah, God is very good, is He not? and I do try to be good. I always try. Sometimes I have said wicked things—once I told a lie. Do you think God will forgive me?"

"God forgives every one. But, Arthur, you know you have been ill; you may have forgotten some of your worst sins. Tell me, my dear, do you remember nothing but what you have told me?"

"Nothing, Norah. Why should I hide anything from you?"

"Then, Arthur, when you pray, ask God to forgive you all those sins which you may have forgotten, but which you would repent if you could remember. Say that now, Arthur, while you think of it, else it may go out of your head."

He put up his trembling hands and repeated.

"Lord, forgive me all the sins that I have forgotten." Then he smiled. "It is all very well, Norah, but I have forgotten nothing."

The past was clean gone, then. Norah sat down on the stool by the fire, and taking his hand in hers, fondled it, while she tried to touch his memory in some point at least. It seemed to her so dreadful that the dying man should go out of the world in a dream, ignorant of the dreadful past which lay between his sunny youth and his bewildered age.

At tea time, Norah observed him pondering apparently over some mighty problem, with knitted brows.

"Norah," he said at last, "I have been thinking of what you said yesterday—about self-denial. Please, no sugar in my tea."

"Why not, Arthur?"

"Because," setting his lips hard, "because sugar is one of the pleasures of life, and I must try to learn to forego them all, if necessary."

He drank his tea unsweetened, and then began to enlarge on the beauties of self-sacrifice. The boy was, if anything, growing younger, not older.

But his time for growing at all was short. He caught a bad cold trying to swim his new boat in the water butt, and was put to bed, and nursed by Norah. Doctors came to see the poor boy thus prematurely threatened, and shook their learned heads. They sent him bottles, and the child took them meekly when Norah persuaded him, making no lamentations over the necessity, but patiently lying in his bed, reading when he was strong enough some pious picture-book which Norah got for him; or, he would talk hopefully of the day when he should be quite well again. A most gentle and pure-hearted boy always.

Accustomed as Norah was to the strange contrast between the boyish ways and the venerable grey hair, she sometimes felt giddy, as if the room were going round as the old man poured out his childish prattle.

As the autumn deepened into winter his weakness increased upon him. Then came a time when he no longer rose from his bed at all, and Norah had to nurse him like the sick child that he was. But he never lost his hopefulness and buoyancy of spirit. Moreover, he had no disease, only a general break up of the great constitution he had ruined by so many excesses;—and through it all the mirth and glee of the boy, which made the sick-room of poor old Cardiff Jack a sweet and pleasant place to go to. Myles and Jack sat with him sometimes, but chiefly it was Norah who, when the old man was laid on his sofa by the fire, brought her work and talked to him of heaven, and God's goodness, and all holy things, so that the youthful mind of her patient was filled with all manner of pleasant visions.

One night he had a bad dream. Norah heard him cry for help, and sprang from her bed, thinking of that other night, only a few months before, when she had battled with the half-maddened old drunkard, now so strangely changed.

His face was flushed, and a look of terror was in his eye.

"Norah," he moaned, catching her hand, "do not leave me, dear Norah, not till I have gone to sleep again. I have had a dreadful dream. I think it must be real. See, Norah,

I thought I broke Lucy's heart, and killed my own mother with some disgrace that came upon me. Norah, I did not cry, or say a single word. I only laughed. Think of it. I dreamed that I had ruined and killed my mother, my dear mother who loves me so. Why does she not come to see me now I am ill and dying? And in my dream I saw Lucy. She was grown up, and she said to me: ' I have loved you always, Arthur, in spite of your wicked selfishness, and your disgrace. I love you still. Let me, now that you have no friends left, be your friend still. ' Let me be your wife, Arthur, if by that I can rescue you from yourself. Take me, marry me, if you like, if only that can help to save you.' Norah, I promised her that I would marry her; and I only took her money and became worse than ever. It is all a dreadful dream. I try to forget it, but I cannot. I had letters from poor Lucy, such kind and loving letters, so full of forgiveness, and I used them all to get more money out of her. Always more money; always more wickedness. And one day another letter came. It told me that Lucy was dead, with a prayer for me; and she sent me a last message that she would give me more money; but I had taken it all, taken it all, Norah. Could you believe it? And what do you think I did? I went away and got drunk. Oh! what a dreadful dream. Why does not Lucy come to me? Oh, bring me Lucy, Norah."

The girl soothed him as much as she could, and presently he fell into a restless slumber. Some chord of his memory had been touched, and the spectres of the past were risen to torment him once more.

He died on Christmas Day—that day when St. Peter leaves the gates open, so that all who die on the blessed birthday may enter freely at the golden portals of heaven.

He was very weak in the morning, and his mind wandered strangely, but always within the narrow limits of his delusion. He was sailing a boat on the river; he was fishing with cousin Lucy; he was running races round the garden with her; he was flying a kite with Lucy, to help tie on the tail; he was telling her stories; he was singing hymns with her. It was pitiful to hear the old man's quavering voice singing tremulously the old hymns that were in fashion fifty years ago, and more, hymns of sadness and despondency—chiefly on the old Wesleyan pattern—or, at best, expressive of the vanity of this world, and the subdued happiness of the next—hymns with none of the unreal rapture which marks the modern utterances. Norah watched him as the hours of morning passed slowly away.

There came a change about noon, a sudden and awful change, for, as if with a single stroke, the old man's face was transformed. Yes, he was no longer a boy; the trustful light of innocence and youth faded instantaneously from his eyes; the sunshine left his face; his forehead clouded over; his cheeks were wreathed with a thousand seams and wrinkles; what had been dimples showed like deep pits of temptation; his lips seemed to swell and grow purple; his chin drooped; his nose swelled and reddened. Arthur Dimsdale was dead, and only Cardiff Jack remained.

Norah, horror-struck, rushed to the bell.

The man awoke and sat up in bed. As Jack's footstep was heard on the stairs he broke into a soliloquy on the badness of the times. If we suppress all the ejaculations but the first, it is in deference to popular opinion, and in violence to our veneration for truth, because the speech was interlarded with oaths. "Damn you and smite you!" he began. The girl shrank back appalled. "Why am I lying here like a useless log when there's work to be done, and money to be got for the asking—only for the asking? Ho! ho! Put Cardiff Jack on the right scent, and trust to him to pull you through. Times bad, mate? They never were anything but bad, to a poor liver-coloured pitiful area sneak like you. Times never are bad for Cardiff Jack. When he isn't up to one dodge he is up to another. You make no bleeding error. Put me down on Newmarket Heath to-morrow, and see what I'll bring you in the evening. Ask Poll. Poll knows what I did at Epsom last week. General Duckett was there with six of his best boys; Liverpool Joe was there with his pardner; Flash Charley was there with his bank notes fluttering about like the leaves of the blessed trees, and Cardiff Jack was there. Ask Poll who did the best. Liverpool Joe's in quod, he is, and his pardner too. Bah!—what's the thimble trick? Hanky-pankey's no good;

fortune-telling's no good; as for nabbing a stray wipe—that was all General Duckett done—and one of his boys caught in the very act, with the wipe in his hand and the pocket-book in his blessed little pocket, and as good as twenty pounds a year lost to the poor old General for ever, because the young 'un 'll be sent to a Reformatory. And Flash Charley ducked for a welsher, and might have been killed only that the bobbies interfered. That's a good day's work for them all, ain't it? Ask Poll what I did. Ask her, I tell you. Lord! how neat and quiet I turned out, and how the bets came in—and how I pocketed the swag in the little tent, and how we bolted, Poll and me, and changed our rig, so that the devil himself wouldn't know his own again. Here's luck, boys! Drink to the health of Cardiff Jack. Cardiff Jack's the King. He's the Prince of begging-letter writers. He's the flash boy of all the gentlemen of the road. If you want a plant, come to Cardiff Jack, and pay him, and he'll put you up to it. Come to . . . . come to . . . ."

Here he paused and trembled and turned white, when he saw Jack come into the room.

"I know you," he said. "Why do you come here? Let me go. Let me get up and go away, I say. Why am I kept prisoner . . . prisoner? What am I a prisoner for? No one saw me do it. I won't confess. Stay," he looked round the room bewildered. "There's nobody here except you, and you're dead, because I murdered you long ago when you were a little boy, a pretty little devil of a little boy; and this girl here, she's nobody. She's always here, I think. I will confess that I drowned you—no one knows anything. Go tell them all if you like. There's no proof. Cardiff Jack's my name, tell them. Bring the bobbies—take me to the Beak. Prove it—if you can. Prove it! Prove it! Prove it!"

His voice rose to a shriek as he fell back exhausted.

"Oh, Jack!" murmured Norah. "What are we to do?"

"Nothing. Nothing can be done. The end is very near, Norah."

She threw herself by the bedside, and prayed aloud.

"Where is the body? Ho! ho! Down at

the bottom of the deep, deep sea. Look for it there. Where are the eyes who saw me do it? Bring them here."

"They are here," said Jack, bending over him. "They are here. Look in them. Do you remember the eyes that looked in yours for a gleam of pity and found none?"

"Ay . . ." he moaned. "They are the eyes. I know them; I remember them."

"You are dying. You will be with God in a very short time. I forgive you; ask God to forgive you too."

He put his hands out before him in a wild and piteous way, and his eyes stared vacantly as he listened to the words that seemed to come to him from the grave, the boundless grave of the ocean where he thought the murdered boy was lying.

"What am I to do? Where am I to go? They are all before me. My mother is here—and Lucy—Lucy."

"They have all forgiven you . . . indeed, indeed, they have," said Norah. "Only ask God to forgive you."

He shook his head. He seemed half to understand.

"No use," he said, "no use;—ah!" and fell back as if smitten with some sudden blow.

They thought he was dead. But it was not so. The pulse beat feebly, and the breathing came slowly, and an hour passed by. As they watched, the lines faded out of the face again, and he became, save for the closed eyes, a boy once more.

"It is always so," said Jack. "He will die peacefully, and you will see him again with his childish smile."

But he awoke again. And Cardiff Jack was gone for ever.

"Norah," Arthur murmured, "I am dying. Dear Norah, I have been a terrible trouble to you. Jack, we shall never sail our boat together, now. I thought it would be hard to die so young. But it isn't, Norah, it isn't. I am going to God. There I shall find my cousin Lucy. You told me, I remember, that I should meet her there. Something has gone wrong with me, and I do not recollect when she died, or how I came here. But never mind that now. Norah . . . will it hurt to die?"

"No, dear Arthur. No. Only say your prayers first. Say what I told you."

"Yes, Norah. God, forgive me all the sins I remember, and all the sins I have forgotten, for the sake of Jesus."

Then his head dropped back.

"Kiss me, Norah," he said. "I don't know how you came to me; but I love you, almost as well as cousin Lucy. Kiss me, dear. . . . It isn't hard to die . . . not hard at all . . . and . . . and" . . . he lifted his head . . . "cousin Lucy—dear Lucy, wait one moment and I will go with you, too, to play in the garden."

They were the last words of Cardiff Jack!

CHAPTER XXIV.

WHEN Bastable went away, Paul Bayliss took to his bed and stayed there. The tumult of his mind made his limbs weary and his eyes heavy. He dragged himself to his bedroom, laid himself with a sigh on the bed, and presently fell into a sleep of unconsciousness, that was not sleep, but nervous exhaustion.

When he awoke it was twelve o'clock and his head was on fire. He moaned in his pain; he rolled himself from side to side in an agony of expectation, that was worse than any bodily pain. Twelve o'clock. It was time that Armstrong should come. Twelve o'clock? Why —even now they might be coming with a warrant to arrest him. But no. Bastable would hold his tongue for his own sake. Even now, though, without Bastable's evidence they might on suspicion summon him before a magistrate, and so disgrace him for ever. It was impossible to rest still with such a thought. He threw the covering from him, and sprang upon the floor. He stood there; he heard voices outside, and a trampling of feet in the passage below. Could it be the constables with the warrant? His teeth chattered, his helpless hands hung at his side, his forehead was wet with the sweat of terror, his pale cheeks grew whiter than the pallor of death, and as his limbs huddled together he fell senseless upon the floor.

But it was no officer with a warrant; it was only Jack Armstrong himself brought to the rich man's room by his footman. The man knocked. As no answer came, he knocked again, and yet a third time. Then he opened the door, and timidly peeped in. His master lay in a heap by the bedside, and from his forehead was oozing the thick red blood. The servant called Armstrong, and without a word the two raised the heavy man from the floor and laid him on the bed.

Jack brought water and washed his forehead.

"He has had a fit," he said. "Don't make

a fuss, don't tell Miss Ella. See, he knocked his head against this corner, and cut himself. But that is nothing. You had better fetch a doctor, quietly."

"No, no doctor," murmured Bayliss, who opened his eyes and roused himself with a great effort. "No doctor—not yet. Is that you, Armstrong? Go away, James, and keep a quiet tongue. Where am I? Ah! I remember. Did I fall out of bed?"

"Don't talk, Mr. Bayliss," said Jack. "You have had a faintness."

"Give me some water. So—I am better already. Lift my head higher—another pillow. That is right. Now I can talk. Sit down, Armstrong, and let us talk—let us talk—not talk?—why, what do I want you to come here for?"

He spoke hurriedly, and looked about the room, the ceiling, everywhere, except in Jack's face.

The servant went out and shut the door. Then Paul Bayliss began again—

"Jack, do you know what day this is? It is the day before Christmas. No—I am not wandering: my mind is clear: and I'm not going to talk a lot of blessed rubbish about the happy Christmas season, because that's humbug. It's a time when the hands get drunk, that's what it is, and a beast of a time, too. But—oh! Jack, I am very ill—I am so ill that I cannot be worse. I am dying, Jack, I am dying."

"Nonsense, Mr. Bayliss. You will very soon get over this."

"Never—never! What was I going to say?"

"You were talking about Christmas, Mr. Bayliss. Will you have a little more water?"

The penitent sinner felt his brain wandering a little, but he made a mighty effort and recovered himself.

"It's the fit, and—and—everything. What was I going to say to you? I remember. To-night will be Christmas Eve. A week after this night, three and twenty years ago, Jack Armstrong, your father died. He was drinking with me in the evening: he went away and drank more. Then .... you know the rest. I am not guilty of his death, Jack."

"He left a single field, Mr. Bayliss, the last remnant of the Armstrong estate."

"Last night, Jack, I saw him again. He was sitting where you are. He looked the same as he did in life, and he reproached me. And to-night he will come again. I know he will come again and look at me as he did last night. And what am I to say to him?"

"If I thought he would come," said Jack, irreverently, "I would sit up with you, in order to ask him one question. I should ask him how you got the title-deeds of his estate."

This was hardly the way to meet the tragedy of the situation, but Jack was in an angry mood. He was certain that Bayliss had forged the deed; and he knew that Bastable had been with him; also it was against the lawyer's advice that he acceded to Paul's letter, and came to see him at all. But Bayliss had worked himself into such an agony of terror, that he thought nothing of Jack's tone, and went on with the uneven current of his own ideas.

"I know he will come again to-night. And he was right, Jack, he was right. I feel it now—now that I am dying. He was quite right. The son of my old partner, the man to whom I owed my start in life, made with borrowed money. I ought to have offered you what you asked. Yes, Jack, now that I am ill—and I think that I shall never get better, I have sent for you to offer you a partnership in the great house of Bayliss, ironmaster—not Bayliss and Company. Plain Paul Bayliss. For your sake, my boy, we will make it Bayliss and Armstrong."

"Mr. Bayliss, I want my own."

"It isn't a mere partnership in the profits of your own discovery, Jack, son of my oldest and best friend, that I offer. It is a full half partnership in the great works of Bayliss, ironmaster. That is due to you; I don't grudge anything, Jack, to the son of my old partner. Share and share alike it shall be. What I make, you shall divide."

"Mr. Bayliss, I want my own."

"When you came to me with that Irish fellow, what did I do? I took you in without a premium. I told them to teach you all there was to be learned. I made a man of you. All you know you have learned from me —all you ever taught yourself was in my works. Confess, Jack, is it not so?"

"Mr. Bayliss, I want my own."

"It will be something to-night, when your poor dead father comes to my bedside, to say to him, 'Johnny, I have done what I could. I taught your boy; I gave employment to the man who brought him up: and now, when the boy has become a man, and has learned all he can learn, I make him my partner—half and half—and I leave him to manage the business.' That will be something to say. That will lay the unquiet spirit of Johnny Armstrong."

Jack Armstrong was startled. Was the man shamming? It would have seemed so, but for the frightful change that twenty-four hours had brought about. The full bright eye rolling about in wildness, with the red and heavy eyelids, the flabby cheeks, the fit that he had witnessed, all told Jack that the man was not shamming. Anything but shamming; and the young man's heart was touched at the sight of his misery.

"You forget, Mr. Bayliss," he said, with the confusion that generally seizes virtue when her enemy meets her in some unexpected manner, "you forget that we have copied your deeds of conveyance, and stopped them at the Bank. The man Bastable has returned. You have seen him."

"Ay, ay; all that is nothing. Bastable be damned! It depends on you, Jack—on you. Take my offer—take it. If I live you will be master, if I die you will not repent having smoothed the last hours of a dying man—perhaps a sinful man."

The young man was silent. What could he say? He came there full of the most uncompromising resolutions. He was not to be coaxed or wheedled; he was not to sacrifice one single point of his claims. And yet here was the man who had done him this wrong, the man whom he had considered the most masterful of all men, lying prostrate and helpless at his feet, craving as a boon everything, save the exposure and disgrace that he was fearing.

"Jack Armstrong," continued Bayliss, "don't be cruel and vindictive. As for your father, he always forgave his enemies. If you kicked him, he would kick you back and think no more of it. If I refused you a partnership, you have brought me to the brink of death, and ought to be satisfied. Take it now, and let us be friends."

"But that does not give me what I demand," said Jack. "I want my estate."

"Is that all? Take the estate; take every rod of land in my possession that Johnny Armstrong once owned. It will only be part of the partnership."

Jack began to waver. Why should he be hard upon this poor frightened creature, brought to bay in a corner, and anxious only to make terms?

"Tell me about that conveyance," he said.

"What conveyance? I know nothing about any conveyance."

"Then I know nothing about any partnership. Listen, Mr. Bayliss. I came here resolved to fight you, whatever might happen. You offer terms. But that will not do. Before I think of terms I must know the truth. Tell me all the truth."

Paul Bayliss turned his face from him, and hid it with the pillow.

"The truth—the truth. If I tell you the truth. What if I do not?"

"Then we will prove it, Mr. Bayliss. The deed on which you raised the money is a forgery. We will prove it with you, not in the witness-box, but in the dock. King of Esbrough you called yourself two days ago; the meanest creature in the town will pity you when we have concluded our case."

"I can die," he moaned, in the recesses of the feathers. "I can die. It is easy to stop it all with a pistol."

"No; you only perpetuate your disgrace, because we proceed all the same, and your name will suffer instead of yourself."

"Jack Armstrong, you are young; you are strong; you are clever; you are fortunate." He sat up in bed now, and clutched the other by the wrist. "You think that nothing will ever make you commit a dishonourable thing. Wait, lad, wait. When you have been toiling for twenty years in vain; when every day plunged you deeper in the mire; and when, after all your troubles, a way of safety shows, with wealth and honour beyond, don't think that you, more than other people, will avoid the temptation. God! how poor I was. God! how I dreaded to go home when my wife sat waiting to nag and gird at me, and my sister to ask me what I had done with all her money—seven hundred pounds it was—and no one to welcome me except my little girl, my dear little Ella. Did I stick at doing what I did? No, Jack, no; and if it were to be done again, I would do it over again. That deed, which I forged—yes, forged; there's nobody here to take the words down—forged, Jack Armstrong, is the word—that deed—give me a little more water. My head is clear again after the fit, and I know what I am saying. That deed started the great Esbrough works; on the strength of that deed I took the Ravendale mines; on the strength of that deed I made Perrymont wake up and work the vein on his own property; on that deed rests the fortunes of all this great place. Where there were fields then, there are terraces and villas; where there were paupers are wealthy families. Where there was misery, is comfort. What did it? That deed did it. Who forged the deed? I, Paul Bayliss, I forged the deed—with this right hand."

The confession seemed to relieve him, and his voice grew firmer and steadier.

"But that deed destroyed my fortune while it made yours."

"You knew nothing. Now I offer you a half of what I am making out of that desperate venture."

"Mr. Bayliss, you ask me to compound a felony."

"I do nothing of the sort," replied the casuist, eagerly. "All I say is this: Bring me the copy you have made of the deed; remove the prohibition on Stewart at the Bank; forget all I have said, and you shall not only be partner, but also sole manager of the great Esbrough Works. I will retire: I am growing old. I shall leave everything to you. Refuse, and you can go your own way. You will not be able to prove your case: Bastable and I can square it. There is nobody else to help you; and though you bring discomfort and suspicion upon me, and create a scandal that will cling for the rest of my days, you will be left alone in the world."

All this seemed very true, and Jack wavered.

"I have told you all, Jack Armstrong, because I know you to be a man of honour. You will not go away to Clifton and tell him what I have confessed to you. You will not act upon words, wrung from me on a bed of sickness. No one will know, no one except you and me. And as for Bastable, if he dares to speak, I will bring him up for defamation, by Gad! for I shall destroy the infernal deed at once."

The stunning effect of the fit was gone off by this time, and the man, though weak in body, was clear and bright in mind.

"They all know," he went on, "how fond I have been of you. There was that speech I made the hands after Norah Cuolahan saved you from them. . . . You have been often at my house. . . . I am a friend of Mr. Fortescue's. . . . You have walked about with my daughter. . . . No one can say but what I've treated you as my own son. There will be nothing strange. Bayliss and Armstrong; it used to be Armstrong and Bayliss, in the old days. . . . We will even make it Armstrong and Bayliss again."

"No . . . no . . ." said Jack, touched by this concession more than by any other.

"And . . . and . . . one thing more, Jack, I've kept it for the last, my boy. I've got a daughter. What you do to me, you do to her. If you disgrace me, you disgrace her. Think of the pleasant evenings you have spent, Norah Cuolahan and you, with her, made pleasant by her. She has been brought up in innocence of all this."

Then there was silence. At last Jack spoke again :

"I accept, Mr. Bayliss. You shall, with as little delay as possible, sign a deed of partnership. I will take all the business that comes from the Esbrough estate—properly my estate; you shall have all that comes from the Ravendale farmed estates; and I shall be the manager of all. Do you accept?"

"I accept, Jack; I accept."

"Do not think that I want to press you. You will give me the benefit of your experience; you will gradually come less often to the works."

"What security can I give you, Jack, that I will keep my promise?"

"None," said Armstrong, loftily. "I want nothing but your word."

"You shall have it," returned Bayliss. "If you will give me, first, the assurance of your forgiveness."

Jack, with some hesitation, and much

blushing, gave him his hand. It was a strange and a wonderful thing, after looking on this man for so long as a Colossus of strength, to find that he was after all only an idol whose feet are of clay.

"If you want the deeds," he said sheepishly, "I will bring them to you, copy and original as well. Write me a note for the manager of the Bank. Clifton will get the prohibition removed at once. It is now half-past twelve. Try and sleep if you can."

"Promise me again that not a word of this shall pass your lips. I know your honour. Mr. Fortescue has told me that he made you, above all, a truthful boy. Promise me."

"I promise, Mr. Bayliss. Not one word shall pass my lips, or the lips of Clifton."

He left him. And when he left the heart of the man was uplifted. He thought nothing of the shame and disgrace of his confession—that was like a bitter pill that had to be swallowed and was now done—it was characteristic of him that the fact of other men, counting Bastable, knowing that he was a forger and a common cheat, oppressed him with no trouble at all. Two would not speak, and the third was powerless. He was safe—that was all; for twelve long years there had been weighing upon him, sometimes with a might almost too heavy to bear, the danger that he was in. It was well to argue as he did that there was no danger. He knew there was peril in every hour, peril at every turn that Armstrong might take, peril from every man who had known his father. And yet, though he had long intended to remove the deeds from the custody of the Bank, deeds as damnatory should they be discovered as any clause in the Creed of St. Athanasius, he had never done so. For the resolution to do so had been generally taken in the dead of night, when the conscience is most reproachful, and had been forgotten in the sunshine of the day, when the man is strongest and his nerves the least shaky.

Now it was all over. There would be no more trembling at shadows; no more dread of an awful future; no more horrible anticipations of collapse and shameful exposure; no more, dreams of ten years long, to be spent in a narrow white-washed cell.

He thought over this and was thankful.

His head was still a little confused with his fall, and with the horror of the night he had passed; but he fell back on the pillow and slept the sleep of the righteous, or at least of the forgiven. Three hours later Jack returned, bearing with him the precious documents.

Mr. Bayliss was still sleeping. His face had not upon it the sweet boyish innocence that might be boasted by poor dying Cardiff Jack; you see he had not gone so far in wickedness, and therefore the reaction was not so strong; but there shone from his countenance a wonderful serenity, which bespoke the peace of the inner man. Armstrong laughed to himself when he saw it. Then he gently roused the sleeper.

"I have brought you the deeds, Mr. Bayliss."

He awoke in a moment and clutched them eagerly. Yes, they were all there, and among them the . . . the fictitious deed, written in his own hand-writing, attesting signatures and all, and the copy taken by Mr. Clifton the lawyer. These two he selected from the rest, and, sitting up in bed, tore into the smallest shreds.

"You are sure, Jack," he whispered, "you are sure . . . you swear to me that there are no other copies?"

"I am quite sure that there are no other copies."

"Put them all into the fire for me—stay, no, I will burn them myself. . . . Jack, I feel better already. Tell all the world, if you like, that we are partners from the New Year; you the working partner, I the sleeping. You shall find that I keep my word. Some men, Jack Armstrong, might round on you, and now that all proofs are destroyed——"

"All proofs are not destroyed."

"Eh? eh? How?"

"At least, we could get the affidavits of Stewart the Bank manager, and of Clifton —and myself—and Bastable. There, Mr. Bayliss, don't be alarmed, we shall have no need of affidavits."

"Not the least, not the least," he replied briskly. "And now, Jack, hear me: I feel better already. I will get up and eat something. My dear boy, my dear boy, I am happier at this moment than ever I have been before. To think that this heap of paper before me, which gave me such a devil of a bit of trouble, was the real means of working your fortune——"

"As well as your own, Mr. Bayliss."

"As well as my own," he rejoined cheerfully. "Why, without it, where should we have been? Where would Esbrough be, now? Where would you be? My dear Jack, son of my best friend, poor Johnny Armstrong, it was a PROVIDENTIAL act, quite Providential. It has made us all rich. Lord! Lord! as the poet says, this deed blessed him that borrowed, as well as the other man who lent. And yet, Jack, the world would find fault with us."

"With you."

"With me. So be it. Between ourselves, Jack, I think that the world would call it ugly names. All the same, if the world saw its way to making a fortune by imitating a deed, and never get punished for it, the world would go and do it. Never doubt that."

He was a little light-headed, and talked fast.

"I do not, sir," said Jack, rather sadly.

"To-morrow is Christmas Day. Let me see you the day after. You shall send Clifton to draw our deeds of partnership. Now, Jack, one stipulation, if I may make it. Your own terms, but not Clifton's. Good-bye, my dear, dear boy. I feel as if I was your second father."

Jack left him. Immediately he was gone Paul Bayliss got out of bed. His legs were still shaky after his fall, and his head queer, but it was with something like youthful vigour that he performed, humming a cheerful air, a fandango or *pas seul* before his cheval glass. A long night shirt reaching to the ankles, and somewhat plentifully besprinkled with blood about the shoulder: a face still pale, a forehead with an open wound upon it. Knees that trembled exceedingly, and fingers that refused to crack in time with the melody, though they went through the motion of cracking—these things lent to the dance a grace and charm quite peculiar. "Paul," the dancer exclaimed in a rapture, falling back exhausted on the bed, "you are a free man at last. But you've had a narrow escape, old boy; and what with your cursed fit, and your almighty funk, it's just as well you had a boy instead of a man to deal with. Why, even that rascal Bastable would have made better terms. He might have taken all the past, and he has taken only half the future."

It so happened that James the footman, anxious about his master's welfare, was hovering about the passage outside the bedroom door. Hearing a noise within, he rapped. Receiving no answer, he opened the door softly. To his amazement, Mr. Bayliss, before the cheval glass and in his night shirt, was dancing an elephantine break-down.

James closed the door noiselessly. Then he crept downstairs to the kitchen with awe-struck countenance, and sank breathless into a chair.

"Soosan," he said, "a glass of beer if you can, and quick, I feel that low. I've seen a dreadful sight!"

They brought him the consoler.

"Master," he said, "have gone off his chump—that's all," he added, with the calmness of despair; "that's all;—off his chump. Don't ask me more. We shall all of us lose our situations."

In the midst of the consternation caused by this announcement the master's bell rang.

"No," said James, "not if I know it—not alone."

"Why," said the under-gardener, a youth of seventeen, but of robust habit, "you aren't afraid, James, sure?"

"Not alone," said James.

"Then I'll go with you," said the boy, arming himself with the poker, which he dropped down his back, in readiness. Mr. Bayliss was dressing, and whistling at the same time in a cheerful manner.

"James . . . you did not tell Miss Ella about my accident."

"No, sir," said James, listening for the following steps of the assistant-gardener, who was making ready with the poker. "No, sir. Mr. Armstrong told me not, sir."

"Mr. Armstrong was quite right. Now ask Miss Ella to give me an early dinner, anything, and as soon as the cook can send it up. I feel better, James, but I haven't eaten anything to-day, and I am hungry. Tol de rol lol. And, James . . . James . . . tol de rol lol . . . tell the butler that I think I shall be better without port to-day. Let him give me a bottle of Piper. Très-sec, James; he may also send up a pint of Roederer for Miss Ella. Tol de rol lol."

At dinner he was full of talk—talked, indeed, too fast—and was kind and affectionate to Ella. After dinner came the Christmas waits. He listened with a religious rapture, which his daughter had never before noticed in him, while the boys and men chanted their noels and their hymns.

"A season of loving kindness, Ella," he said. "'God rest you, merry gentlemen, let nothing you dismay, . . . nothing you dismay' . . . Good tidings indeed, and worthy of Christmas eve. A time of general rejoicing. I wish I felt strong enough for a bottle of port. Send out the waits something to drink, and some money, my dear. 'God rest you, merry gentlemen, let nothing you dismay.' What a beautiful time Christmas is! I feel, Ella, as if I never properly appreciated Christmas before. A time of great thankfulness. I shall go to church to-morrow, my dear, and I think I shall stay sacrament. I believe they have it on Christmas day. 'God rest you, merry gentlemen, let nothing you dismay.'"

CHAPTER XXV.

"Children," said Myles, "half our time is made up of forgivin' little wrongs. Why not forgive the big ones as well? I knew Paul Bayliss well in the old days—no one better. He was a good-hearted fellow, and just because he was so poor, he lost his courage. There's nothing tries a man like misery, except riches. Paul Bayliss has had both. He was first poor and then rich. Let Jack take his own again, even if it is not in the way that he would best like. It isn't like a good honest fight at the fair, where a man or two is kilt and it's all over. This is a different kind of fight, and I don't understand it. But that's the girl, the purty creature, Norah; you couldn't turn against the blue-eyed beauty that's so often put her arms round your neck and kissed you so beautiful.

"No, father," said Norah, "I forgot Ella. I was thinking only about Jack and what he should do. Only, if there was no Ella, I should have liked Jack to step into his own, and for all the world to know that he was come to his own again."

"Let things be thus," said Myles. "And now, children both, we must forget that we know anything against Paul Bayliss at all, at all. Whatever he says or does, Norah, never let him know that Jack has told us a single word. I've known men trade in a secret. I've known them sell their silence a hundred times over. Our Cardiff Jack—poor fellow!— once lived a couple of years on a secret, till the man it belonged to could bear it no longer, and blew out his own brains to get quit. Let us hold our tongues. And now, Norah, alaunah, sing us a Christmas hymn before we have our tea."

In the evening Jack went to see Clifton, while Myles sat reading the Bible. This evening he found himself among the minor prophets, and read on, chapter after chapter, in a fine frame of religious bewilderment.

"'Tis a blessed thing, Norah," he said, looking up, "being a Prodesdan. If I'd been a Catholic I should never have opened the book at all; and it's great readin', if you only knew what it meant."

"What book are you reading, father?"

"Sure it's the Bible, asthore. Listen now, 'Woe unto you, Moab!' Who was Moab, I wondher? They were a terrible pair, Norah darlin', they two—Moab and Edom."

"Let me find you a place you will like better, dear father."

"No, thank you, my dear," he returned. "I like it all alike; and I think I've read enough for one day." Here there was a knock at the door. It was Keziah Bastable, breathless and excited. Norah went out to see her.

"Miss Norah, let me speak to you a moment. Come here—to the door. Oh! Miss Norah," she whispered, "Jenny's going on like a mad woman. She's got a knife, and she swears she will have Jack Armstrong's blood, and she's waiting on the door-steps for him, because she saw him go out. What shall I do, Miss Norah?"

Norah hesitated.

"She says she'll kill him, and I can't keep her quiet."

"I will go over," said Norah, after a moment.

"You can't go, my dear young lady. When Jenny's took too much, Jenny's more rampagious than words can tell. I can manage her most times, but I can't manage her then. No one can."

"I am not afraid of her," said Norah, drawing herself up. "Do you think she will kill me?" The tall young Irish girl, fearless, and as strong as if she had been brought up in the wilds of Connemara, looked down in the face of her visitor with flashing eyes.

"I think you are afraid of nothing, Miss Norah," said Mrs. Bastable. "Stay, there's one thing—I've told you most things, but I haven't told you all. If the worst comes to the worst, tell her that . . ." here she dropped her voice to a whisper, "And that you know it."

Norah heard and flushed; then a look of proud contempt fell upon her cheeks.

"And she dared . . . she dared . . ."

"Jack didn't know, my dear."

Norah crossed the road.

Mrs. Bastable went to find Myles.

"Come out, Mr. Cuolahan," she said. "Come out and watch, or there may be mischief. Your daughter's gone to see Mrs. Merrion."

"Norah gone to . . ."

"Yes, and you must come too, or there may be murder done. Come quietly."

The front door at Laburnum Cottage was wide open, and they stole softly together up the steps, and stood outside the doors of Mrs. Merrion's drawing-room, where they heard the voices of Norah and the fair chatelaine, the one firm, clear, and steady; the other rising and falling like the unquiet breeze of a wild October day.

Mrs. Merrion was standing on the highest door-step, looking down the road for the figure of the man she proposed to kill. The winter wind blew her long yellow tresses from her head, and as it was impossible in the moonlight to be sure that they were dyed, they streamed behind her like the golden locks of Velleda. Her attitude of eager expectation, resolute, unstudied, was that of a cat waiting patiently her opportunity to spring: her right hand held a long sharp knife, half concealed by the folds of her dress: her arms were bare: she wore a low dress, showing the white shoulders of which she was so proud. With the excitement of her wrath there had come back to her something of the brightness of her youth, and, tigerish as was her attitude, no one in Esbrough had ever seen her so beautiful as in this hour of anticipated revenge. Even in the days of nursery-governesshood, and sweet maidenly loveliness, Jenny was not so graceful, so bright-eyed, so lovely as on this Christmas evening, long after her beauty had been worn by the winters.

Suddenly she saw, standing before her— Norah. The girl, sensible of the danger she might encounter at the hands of a woman half mad with jealousy, did not assume the attitude dear to the imagination of strong-minded ladies who make speeches, and, impelled by a natural admiration of qualities not possessed by themselves, love to picture gentle womanhood clothed in her own meekness and innocency. Far from it. Norah was quite prepared, even for an assault, and she was not afraid of it. As she stood before the yellow-haired fury, her hands were free for action, and her eyes ready to catch the exigencies of the situation. She was, to begin with, in case the fury should assail her, a good head taller than her antagonist, and she had the strength of ten Jennys.

"What do *you* want here?" cried Mrs. Merrion, instinctively hiding the knife. "Why do you come to me? Have you not done mischief enough to me? I hate you. I hate you for your pretended goodness. . . . I hate you for taking Jack away from me."

"It is cold in the open air," said Norah, calmly; "shall we talk inside?"

She passed by her, regardless of her hot breath and flaming eyes. Mrs. Merrion followed her without a word.

Keziah and Myles planted themselves outside the door and listened, waiting for any sounds of violence. But there were none.

"You want to say something about Jack," Mrs. Merrion began. "Very well, say it, if you please, and go." She threw herself into a chair, and assumed the attitude of a listener. She was ashamed of the knife in her hand, too, and wanted to hide it.

"Go on, Countess of Connaught," she

sneered. "Countess of Connaught? Kitchen-maid of Connaught. If I'd known you were coming, I'd have got out the Irish whisky. Take a chair, if you like, and go on."

This was very fine, but it had the disadvantage of being vulgar, and therefore out of place. The best things are sometimes thrown away by this kind of carelessness.

"I am going on, Mrs. Merrion," Norah replied. "First, had you not better put down that knife? It is dangerous."

Oblivious for the moment that it was a knife she had in her hand, Mrs. Merrion was fanning herself with the edge. She threw it on the floor impatiently.

Norah did not take a chair. She stood. This gave her an advantage over the enemy. Her face was calm and her eyes grave. There was a look of resolution in them which daunted Mrs. Merrion.

"I am come to finish your threats against Mr. Armstrong. You have certain letters of his."

"Hundreds."

"You will give them all to me, at once."

"Will I?"

"And you will leave this place altogether, in two days."

"Shall I?"

"I am come here on purpose to tell you this. I should have come to-morrow, but I heard you were threatening wild things, so I came to-night."

"Jack is afraid to come, actually afraid to come, and so he sends his last new sweetheart."

"Will you please give me the letters?"

"No, I will not." Mrs. Merrion sprang to her feet. "I will not. How dare you ask for Jack's letters? Give you the letters? They shall be read in open court. All the world shall know——"

"Who and what Mrs. Merrion is."

Adelaide, or Jenny, turned pale for a moment.

"I know everything."

"Leave the room!" said Mrs. Merrion, with dignity; "leave my house!"

"Shall I show you that I know what and who you are? Listen. You were a nursery-governess; by name, Susan Jane. You left off being nursery-governess—but I will not tell you why. You never were married to any General Merrion at all; but I will spare myself and you the rest of your story, unless you force me."

"I will not give up Jack's letters. I will die first."

"Then to-morrow all the town will know your history, and if you bring an action against him, you shall have to tell, yourself, in open court, what that history is. You know best how you will stand that ordeal. Give me the letters and leave this place. Perhaps in the next town you go to no one will know it."

Norah stopped, because there was no need of more. It was an easy victory. Mrs. Merrion collapsed suddenly. Then, as unable to control her tears as her wrath, answered with a passionate fit of crying—

"Oh! I love him," she lamented, "I love him. You don't understand how I love him. Jack, with his brown hair, and his bonny eyes, and his sweet voice—oh! Jack, Jack, I wish I had died before I met you. Why was I born? What have I done? I was so happy before you came."

"Where are the letters?" Norah asked calmly, with no anger or irritation in her voice, but only that cold resolution which subdued her rival.

Jenny pointed to the davenport, and fell in a heap on the floor, weeping and sobbing.

Norah opened it. There was a bundle of letters so thick that her heart sank within her. They were tied up and superscribed, "All Jack's letters."

"Norah, leave me one," cried the woman.

But Norah would leave none at all. She put the whole bundle together in her pocket.

"Come, Mrs. Merrion," she said kindly, "you will forget all this trouble, and you could never have married him."

Mrs. Merrion rose slowly. She wiped her eyes, composed her face, and closed the desk.

"I want no pity," she said. "You have forced me to give up the letters. I shall leave this miserable town. Tell Jack that he will never see me again. And now go."

Norah left.

Outside the door she found her father and Keziah.

"Come, father," she said, "this is not a place for us to stay in."

·Keziah shut the door and put up the chain. Then she went back to her cousin prepared for a scene.

But there was no scene. Jenny was quite calm and composed.

"Come in, Keziah," she said sweetly. "Don't be terrified, my dear. Pick up that knife and put it away. I suppose I was mad after dinner. I sometimes am, I know, and then I do silly things, and frighten people. That was why you fetched over that Norah girl."

"Yes, Jenny, that was the reason."

"Well, never mind. I don't know what made me such a fool about that boy Jack Armstrong. He's a handsome lad; but you were right, cousin: he is too young for me. I've paid him out, though, because I've given all his letters to Norah. Fancy her reading them all through, every word. Won't she let him have it in the morning? And when they're married and things go wrong, won't she throw them in his teeth? I rather think, Keziah, his dearest Adelaide will be a rod in pickle for Master Jack to the end of his natural days. She'll lay it on, or I'm mistaken in her character. And as for him, I'm glad of it. It serves him right."

But it was not a rod in pickle at all. Jenny thought and spoke after the manner of her kind; Norah acted after the manner of hers. That is, she gave the letters to Jack without looking at so much as the signature to a single one.

CHAPTER XXVI.

"And now, Keziah," Mrs. Merrion said, drawing on her gloves, "I am going to do a great stroke of work. You will get in all the bills and pay them. You will tell the landlord that I am going away; you may arrange to sell all the heavy furniture. We shall flit, cousin Keziah; we shall go back to London. Ah! the dear old place! I shall be home to luncheon. Kidneys sautés, my dear."

She drove straight to Mr. Bayliss's works. The great man was not there; then she laughed, and drove to his house. Paul Bayliss received her card with a curious expression. Ella was in the garden, or somewhere out of the way, for which he felt grateful, and he ordered the lady to be taken into his own study.

He found her dressed as Mrs. Merrion knew

how to dress—her seal-skin jacket and bright ribbons showing off the fulness of her charms, and the delicate colours artistically displayed upon her fair cheeks. Her eyes, touched with a little bismuth, presented the appearance of recent tears. This was a very effective stroke.

"Adelaide!" said the great man. "This is unusual. And crying! What has happened?"

"You do not want me in your house. You come to mine: you can come to the poor young widow and—and steal away her heart."

"Adelaide! Pray explain yourself."

"My late husband's brother has written to me. He wants me to go out to Baltimore. I am come here to know what I am to say."

"Say, Adelaide! Why, go by all means."

"And will you come after me—all that way?"

"Why, no. I hardly think——"

"I don't understand you, Mr. Bayliss. Do you mean that you have meant nothing all the time?"

"Why—really—Adelaide! We have had our little dinners and our pleasant evenings; but what more could I mean? You could not imagine that I was going to propose marriage."

"Could not imagine, sir!—could not imagine!" The blue eyes flashed frenzy, as she threw back the veil from her face, and disclosed the golden tresses yet humid with the recent dye. "Could not imagine! Did you actually dare to come week after week to my house—the home of the widow of a Confederate General Officer, and dupe me with promises of undying affection, and then turn round upon her and say it was all pretence! Do you dare to say you meant nothing that day when I let you—I blush to own it—let you kiss my cheek! Oh, Hector Washington Merrion!—if you were alive you would kill this man, as you killed the Northerner Colonel at Baltimore, because he dared to drink my health in Bourbon whisky at a bar."

She sat down, and putting her handkerchief to her eyes, shed copious floods of tears, or at least seemed to do so to the elderly lover.

"My dear Ad—Adelaide."

"Oh, Paul! Paul! how many more women's hearts are you going to break?"

He smiled. It is perhaps not unpleasant

at fifty-five to be reminded that you are yet able to break many women's hearts.

"Adelaide, if I had known——"

"As if you could not have known. As if you could have thought that I, a poor weak, innocent creature, trustful to a fault, as the poor dear General always used to say, could be with you, and hear you, and even—even—oh, Paul!"—here she hid her face—"even kiss you, without thinking—without feeling sure—oh, Paul! my heart will break, and I wish I could die."

The symptoms became alarming. Paul took her hand.

"My poor Adelaide—my dearest Adelaide——"

"He calls me dearest," she murmured; "and yet he means nothing."

"If I could calm you—soothe your feelings, my poor sensitive girl—soothe yourself."

"I cannot—I cannot. It is too cruel!"

"Let us talk it over, Adelaide. Be reasonable, my dear. It is true that I—I love you," he made a great gulp. "But consider, I am an old man."

"No, Paul, no; not old."

"And you are a young woman—a very young woman."

She gave a little murmur of acquiescence.

"I am, besides, a widower. And I have a daughter. How, Adelaide, I ask, how could I ask that daughter to accept a second mother, not much older than herself?"

"You should have thought of all that before, Mr. Bayliss."

"True, I should; but, Adelaide, you are the cause. Look at yourself in the glass, and ask yourself why."

"Paul Bayliss, this is folly. Tell me in plain terms—will you marry me?"

"No, I will not, Mrs. Merrion. That is in plain terms, is it not?"

She shook him off, and stood up, flinging back her drapery with a gesture that meant business.

"Then, Mr. Bayliss, there is but one course open to me. My London lawyer has been with me to-day." This was a fib, but Paul Bayliss changed colour. "He has read your letters. He advised me, Paul Bayliss, to bring the case before a court of law;—with damages, I think he said. What does that mean?" she added innocently.

"Well, ma'am, I suppose you know, in spite of your crafty looks," Bayliss replied, "damages mean money. You want to extort money from me, do you? Come, how much?"

"My lawyer," replied the lady, looking modestly on the ground, "said that you were a very rich man, and must pay for your amusements. Pretty amusement, to break a woman's heart."

"We've heard that before, Mrs. Merrion. Let us stick to business. And your lawyer thinks that with damages we might heal the wound?"

"You are cruelly sarcastic, Paul. He said ten thousand pounds."

"Ten thousand devils! Do you imagine, madam, that I am going——"

"Or else we would go into court with all our letters, and show Mr. Bayliss in his true colours—the gay Lothario! Oh, Paul! it will be a dreadful thing to me, but a far more dreadful thing to you. Think of your philanthrophy, my poor Paul, and your character for common sense, and your grand position in the town, and the respect in which all men hold you: think of that, and then see how awful it will be to stand up and hear all the letters read, one after the other. Oh, Paul! my heart bleeds for you."

Paul Bayliss pronounced a great and mighty oath.

"Don't swear," said the lady, "because you are a churchwarden, and it's wrong."

He swore again.

"Paul Bayliss, it is a pity we should quarrel. Look here, now; I would willingly spare you annoyance, but I cannot possibly overlook your conduct. You *must* be punished somehow, Paul. It is bad for me to lose a rich husband, and so good a man as everybody says you are—very bad; but it is worse for you to let all the world know how you have treated a woman who trusted you. Shall Keziah Bastable go into the witness-box and tell of the little dinners that she used to cook for you every week? Keziah does not love you, my poor Paul. She remembers you when you were quite a poor man. She has often amused herself by telling me how you used to borrow Johnny Armstrong's money and wear his clothes, and how you had to make your wife do the housework because you were too poor to keep a servant. She told me once, but this I hardly believe, that you used at one time to take copying-work from a lawyer, and keep the accounts for the church, where her father was sexton and parish clerk. She will take a delight, this malicious Keziah, in telling all the world these, among other, painful things. Oh! Paul, could you not even remember the prawn curries I used to give you with the Bombay ducks, and the pudding you were so fond of, flavoured with vanille! Have you forgotten my clear mulligatawny? Did you ever taste red mullet with such a sauce as mine? Where will you get the *bouillabaisse* that I alone know how to make? And think of the mayonnaise. Paul, there is still half-a-dozen of the dry champagne left, and four bottles of the Château margaux besides; and at least two dozen of the Corton. You gave them to me. You would like to send for them back again, perhaps? The Curaçoa and the Chartreuse are nearly all gone, and——"

"Confound the Curaçoa!" said Paul.

Mrs. Merrion sat down, and began to cry again.

"Stop it, Adelaide," said Paul. "My lawyer shall see you. We will buy you off; we will silence you, somehow."

"I am going to London, Mr. Bayliss," said Mrs. Merrion. "Oh! Paul, what dreams of happiness have been shattered! Go; make love to some more fortunate woman. Let her believe you, if she can. Marry whom you will, and when you are tired of her, come back to your Adelaide, and you shall find the same mul—mul—mulligatawny, clear, and the same prawn curry, with the Bombay ducks."

She threw herself into his arms.

At that moment the door opened, and Mr. Clifton, the lawyer, came in. It was an interesting tableau. Mr. Bayliss, with a very red face, was trying to push from him the clinging form of the disconsolate dame, while she, one hand round his burly neck, was staunching the tears that seemed to flow from her pearly eyes with her pocket-handkerchief in the other hand.

"There—get off—leave me alone. Mr. Clifton, for God's sake shut that door. If Ella were to see. Go away, Adelaide—I mean

Mrs. Merrion. Take her away, Mr. Clifton—take her away!"

It so happened that Jack had only that morning communicated to Clifton the true history of his own imbroglio with the fair widow, so that the bystander looked on with an expression of the keenest enjoyment.

But he had the presence of mind to interfere.

"Pray, Mrs. Merrion," he said.

"You are witness, sir. I call you to witness," the lady cried, with an astonishing alacrity, "that you have seen Mr. Bayliss embracing me."

"Pardon me, madam," he replied; "I am Mr. Bayliss's lawyer, and can see nothing."

It was a bold stroke on the young solicitor's part. Bayliss caught at the expression.

"My lawyer, Mrs. Merrion. He will call and arrange with you. Take her away; do take her away."

Mr. Clifton led the weeping lady from the room, and Bayliss sunk back in a chair, wiping the signs of emotion from his brow.

Mrs. Merrion left her conductor at the door, and refused his further escort.

Outside the door a new thought struck her. She took the way to Captain Perrymont's.

The captain, after an hour or two at the laboratory, was preparing to visit his works. He greeted Mrs. Merrion with a cheery salute.

"Aha, Mrs. Merrion! Come to see an old sailor? Shake hands, shake hands."

"This is not a visit of ceremony, Captain Perrymont."

"So much the better, so much the better. Glad my son is not at home, though. Must keep the young fellow out of mischief, you know. Might fall in love with blue eyes and yellow hair—eh? Not a usual combination, and, consequently—fetching. Every woman ought to aim like you, my dear Mrs. Merrion, and turn art to the improvement of nature."

"If you mean, Captain Perrymont, that I dye my hair——"

"My dear madam, what a cruel thing to say! Dye your hair, indeed! 'The yellow hair that Julia wears is hers, and who denied it! I know 'tis hers, and this I know, for I learned how she dyed it.' Martial, ma'am—freely imitated."

"Captain Perrymont, you are a wretch!"

"They used to tell me so thirty years ago, Mrs. Merrion; but I was younger then. Now I'm getting old, and I'm a wretch in another sense."

"You came and stole your letters, Captain Perrymont—the letters in which you promised to marry me!"

"Ho! ho! ho!" said the captain, laughing till his lean body shook all over. "The best stroke of business I ever did. I burned them, every one, Adelaide."

"You villain! And you call yourself a gentleman, I suppose?"

"I do, indeed, Mrs. Merrion; and an old fool to boot."

"My lawyer has been with me this morning, Captain Perrymont."

"I'm devilish sorry for you, ma'am. I am, indeed. That's two guineas at least gone, and nothing to show for it."

"He advises me, Captain Perrymont, to bring the case before a court of law."

"Does he indeed, Mrs. Merrion?"

"Will you keep your promise, and marry me?"

"I never made you a promise to marry you, and I will not marry you."

"Then I will bring an action."

"Bring a dozen, madam."

"Unless you consent to a compromise, Captain Perrymont. Dreadful as it is to my feelings, I am sure he is right, and I must not—I cannot—look over your shameful behaviour."

"Don't look it over, Mrs. Merrion. Look under it or any other way. And now, ma'am, I'm a sailor, and yet I am not quite a fool. *Do* you think that at my time of life I am going to pay black mail?"

"Upon my word, Captain Perrymont," Jenny replied, with admiration, "I believe you are the only man among them all."

"Don't know what you mean, Adelaide."

"Let us have peace. Look here, my old salt," her tone dropped easily into the colloquial English affected by ladies slightly below the rank of life into which generals of the army usually marry, "let us be friends. Now I'm going to leave this stupid old place and go back to London. Why I ever came here I do not know. And you will call upon me, will you?"

" Will I, Adelaide? Of course I will. And I'll come up to London on purpose. What a witch it is! I say, Adelaide," here he dropped his voice to a whisper, " I suppose it's all bunkum about the Confederate General, isn't it ? "

" Come and dine with me in London," she returned, laughing, and showing her white teeth. "And, Captain," she laid her hand on his arm, and looked up in his face with a sentimental sigh, "send me some more of that old port, will.you? It is little indeed that I am able to take myself, but that Keziah has drank it all up."

Only Clifton and Mr. Bayliss know the awful sum which the latter paid to keep Mrs. Merrion quiet. The latter swears still whenever he thinks of it. It was indeed an excellent morning's work, and Jenny took her *rognons sautés* for luncheon with unusual relish after it.

CHAPTER XXVII.

In the good old days, when the play had a dozen scenes instead of three, as at present, the scene before the last was always a short "carpenter's scene." This is my carpenter's scene.

After the departure of Mrs. Merrion, Paul Bayliss had another visitor. He walked in without the ceremony of sending in a card, and grasped the great man's hand with an easy familiarity, which would have made the footman's calves to dissolve. He even kept the hand in his own and pressed it with the fervour of old friendship.

"What cheer, mate?" he asked. "Hearty? That's right! Two days ago you were all in the doldrums, glass down, rainy weather, no breeze aft, breakers ahead—eh? That's what they say abroad. Lord! I learned the sailor's talk when I sailed from California to

Honolulu; and nothing done when I got there—waste of time, governor, like everything else. But there, everything works round for the best; and now you've got Doctor Bastable, old Ben Bastable, who knows all the secrets of Nature, and a good many that ain't quite what might be called Nature—you'll be all right. Bless you! I practised physic out in the west for a year, till the editor lost his two children and his wife under my treatment, he said; then I had to dig out. Now let's go into this little difficulty."

"What little difficulty, Mr. Bastable?"

Paul Bayliss was a very big man, and, standing on his hearthrug, while his visitor sat on a low chair almost at his feet, had very considerably the advantage.

"Difficulty? Why, man alive, what should I mean?"

"Pray explain yourself, Mr. Bastable."

Benjamin Bastable began to perceive that there was something unexpected. The approach of misfortune is like that of rain, heralded always by a cold wind.

"I mean," he said, dropping his voice to a whisper, "I mean, the deed."

"What deed?"

"I mean the forgery, then," he cried, springing to his feet, "if you will have it."

Bayliss met it with a front of brass.

"Forgery!—what forgery?"

"What forgery? Yours, man. Yours, yours, yours. Do you hear?—your forgery of my name!"

"Bastable, you rave, or you are drunk. Explain yourself."

For an answer Bastable seized his hat and rushed out of the house.

He ran, swearing like an American skipper, to the office of young Clifton, the lawyer.

"I've seen him," he said, "the old fox. I've seen him, and he tries to back out. But I will be even with him. Do what you like, sir. Proclaim it in all the streets, and I will swear to it. The deed's a forgery."

"What deed, Mr. Bastable?"

"What you showed me . . . . Oh, Lord! oh, Lord! Here's pretty villainy."

"I showed you a paper with some writing. I asked you if a certain name was in your hand."

"Did man ever hear the like?" cried the

bewildered Benjamin. Bit by bit he told his tale.

Mr. Clifton was young, but he had the craft and subtlety of the serpent, therefore he assumed the tone of virtue.

"So, sir, you left us under the impression that you had discovered a forgery, out of which you could make capital, did you? You went to Mr. Bayliss, hoping to buy his silence, and you find you cannot. And where is your forgery? Upon my word, sir, you are likely to get yourself in a very pretty scrape."

The man sat on a chair, and dropping his hat on the floor, looked volumes—intricate and unintelligible volumes; treatises of metaphysics.

"What will you do now, Mr. Bastable?"

"I've been tricked."

"On the contrary, you wanted to trick others. Now, sir," Clifton shook an ominous fore-finger in his face, "dare to repeat, outside, what you have said here, and you shall have two years for libel."

"It's hard," said Bastable. "I made his fortune; I found the iron for him."

"And now you accuse him of a crime. Mr.

Bayliss has no further cause, at any rate, for gratitude. Come, Bastable, I suppose you are hard up. Suppose I advance you a trifle to go away with?"

"Aha! you want me to go."

"Or suppose I bring you up for deserting your wife, eh? I can get a warrant out in half an hour."

"How much?" said the worthy logician, after a few moments of calm argument in his own bosom. "It's a rummy ramp—but how much?"

It is the last scene: the scene in which there is little to say but plenty to look at.

A gigantic banquet. A supper to all Mr. Bayliss's workmen, given by himself on New Year's Day. He takes the chair. On his right is Jack Armstrong: on his left is Mr. Fortescue: Captain Perrymont, Frank Perrymont, and the notables are at the high table: below sit the thousand workmen.

They drink the health of the master. Presently he rises. He is big and burly; he looks a master every inch; he is loud-voiced, jovial, and confident.

He makes the best speech of his life; he reminds the men how fifteen years back Esbrough had been but a miserable market town; how the desolate beach had no docks; how the streets had no life, and in a sudden burst of eloquence he called upon them to look at the town he had himself erected. He took all the credit to himself—every bit. He was the father of the town—the founder of the modern Chicago.

"But, my friends," he went on, "I am growing old. Besides, I have a duty to fulfil. Here sits one"—he laid his hand on Jack's shoulder—" whom you all know. Whose son is he?—Johnny Armstrong's! Who were the Armstrongs? You Esbrough men know that here sits the last descendant of the race. It is right that in the risen fortunes of the place which once his people owned, he himself should have a share. And what share? The share that I, his father's partner in less prosperous times, can give him. Friends all, here is your new master. Jack Armstrong is king; I resign. Leave me the evening of my days for good works. The firm will be as of old, 'Armstrong, Bayliss, and Co.' Henceforth I come to the works as a visitor only."

There was dead silence for a few moments, and then a great shout! In the midst of it rose an old man, Jack's first doctor, and held up his hand.

"Jack Armstrong's health," he cried, in a voice that did credit to septuagenarian lungs. "Stop one moment. I propose it because I am the man who saw him first. In the factory he was born, with the flames of the furnace for the first light that he saw; in the factory he has lived; in the factory he shall go on working. He is our child—an Esbrough man!—and we are proud of him. Drink all, after me—Health and happiness and prosperity to —THIS SON OF VULCAN."

THE END.